GARHWAL HIMALAYA

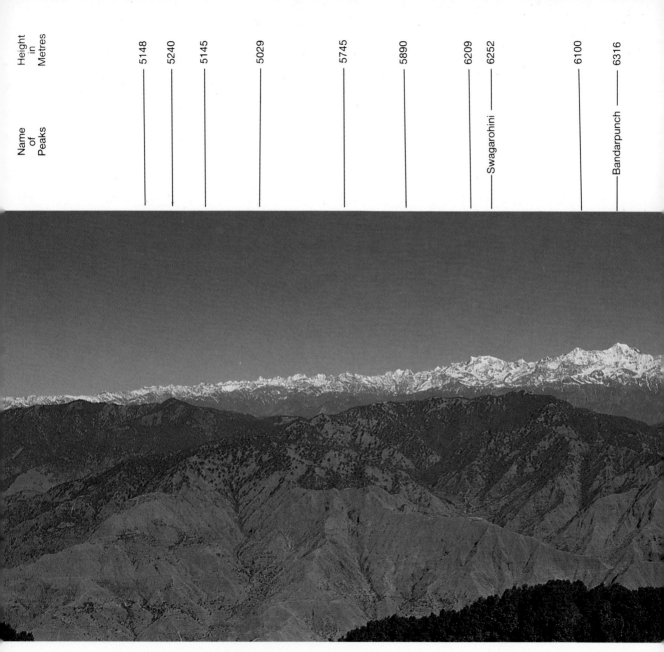

Height in Metres	Name of Peaks
5148	
5240	
5145	
5029	
5745	
5890	
6209	
6252	Swagarohini
6100	
6316	Bandarpunch

From Toap Tibba Mussoorie

Cover—View of Thalesagar peak over the waters of Kedar Tal (5000 m). Thalesagar is 6904 m. The peak to the left is Bhrigu Parvat (elevation 6772 m). They are in the Gangotri region.

Snow View: View from Toap Tibba 6 km from Mussoorie along the Tehri road.

Bhartkhunta ——— 6578
Kedarnath ——— 6940
Kharcha Kund ——— 6613
Satopanth ——— 7075
Chaukhamba or ——— 7138 / 7068 / 6974
Badrinath Peaks ——— 6853
Nilkanth ——— 6957
Daula ——— 5955
——— 7077
Dunagiri ——— 7066
Chang Bang ——— 6863
——— 6636
Nanda Devi ——— 7817

TO SOUTH-EAST

Approx. 500 km

6075 —— Srikanta 6133 —— Gangotri 6672 —— 6599 —— Jaonli 6632 —— Sonero Parvat 6904

VIEW OF GARHWAL HIMALAYA FROM NORTH-WEST

GARHWAL HIMALAYA

By
Gurmeet & Elizabeth Thukral

Introduction
Comdr. Jogindar Singh

FRANK BROS. & CO. 285/=

First published in 1987 by
FRANK BROS AND COMPANY (PUBLISHERS) PVT LTD, NEW DELHI
in collaboration with
K C ANG (PUBLISHING) PTE LTD, SINGAPORE

REPRINTED 1989

Layout and design by Elizabeth Thukral

Phototypeset in Fournier by
Spantech Publishers Pvt Ltd, New Delhi 110008

Printed in the Republic of Singapore by Kin Keong Printing Co. Pte Ltd.

For
Sarah Shakuntla

Contents

List of Maps

Elevations of Important Places

Agoda	2286 m	Ghansyali	976 m	Ramni	1982 m
Ali Buggial	3350 m	Gopeshwar	1300 m	Ransi	2266 m
Alneha Pass	3667 m	Guptakashi	1319 m	Reeh	2134 m
Auli	3049 m	Gwaldam	1329 m	Rishi Tal	5000 m
Bansi Narayan	3400 m	Hanuman Chatti	2400 m	Rudragaira	5518 m
Bhagirathi I	6556 m	Helang	1060 m	Rudranath	3559 m
Bhagirathi II	6512 m	Hem Kund	4150 m	Sarson Patal	5000 m
Bhagirathi III	6454 m	Jhala	2439 m	Saurikigad	1218 m
Bhairo Chatti	2439 m	Kaliani	2683 m	Senatoli	4265 m
Bhrigu	6772 m	Kalpeshwar	2134 m	Shilla	1988 m
Bhujgara	4000 m	Kalyani	1829 m	Shivling	6543 m
Bodni Buggial	3354 m	Kamet	7756 m	Silisamudar	5020 m
Budhakedar	1524 m	Karna Prayag	788 m	Sonprayag	1829 m
Chamoli	960 m	Kauri Pass	4265 m	South Base	5338 m
Chandra Shilla	3930 m	Kedardome	6831 m	Sudarshan Parbat	6507 m
Chang Bang	6864 m	Kedarnath	3584 m	Swargarohini	6252 m
Chuna Chatti	1463 m	Kedar Tal	5000 m	Taluka	1900 m
Deodhi	3668 m	Khatling	3658 m	Tapovan	4463 m
Deoria Tal	2440 m	Khatling Glacier	3719 m	Tehri	770 m
Darshan Tal	4572 m	Lata Kharak	4000 m	Thalesagar	6904 m
Dharmshala	3500 m	Maggu	3049 m	Tharal;	333 m
Dharansi	4667 m	Malla	1478 m	Trijugi Narayan	1982 m
Dibrugheta	3668 m	Maser Tal	3675 m	Trishul	7142 m
Debal	1218 m	Nanda Gunti	6309 m	Uttarkashi	1158 m
Dodhi Tal	3024 m	Nandanvan	4400 m	Valley of Flowers	3658 m
Dumak	2733 m	Narayan	1982 m	Vasuki Tal (Panch Kedar)	4150 m
Gangi	2591 m	Pangrana	2073 m	Vasuki Tal (Gangotri Region)	4900 m
Gangotri	3046 m	Panwalikanta	3963 m	Wan	2439 m
Gauri Kund	1981 m	Phyalu	2286 m	Yamunotri	3185 m
Ghat	1331 m	Purola	1524 m	Yamunotri Pass	5670 m

FOCUS

As a child growing up in the foothills of the Himalaya I often went on treks, which grew longer as I grew older. In preparation for these treks I often felt the need for a single comprehensive guide to the Garhwal area, my main stomping ground. Usually I combined the resources at hand (several outdated books) with personal accounts and then set out and hoped for the best. Although this book is not as comprehensive as many Alpine journals and guides, it does give the basic information necessary for the intelligent trekker to work from. Any special problems for the trekker have been noted. As much as I may wish otherwise, I have been unable to travel along all the trekking routes personally. Particularly the Nanda Devi sanctuary which is now a protected area, Kuari Pass, the ridge connecting Har-ki-dun (Osla) and Yamunotri and the Gangotri-Kedarnath yatra route: the information for these have been collected from personal accounts.

This book is the work of several people, not the least my wife, Elizabeth, co-author, editor and designer. Also I must acknowledge Bill Aitken who shared his expertise not only by writing several articles but also in many question/answer sessions. Arun Sanon has also been a source of knowledge of the ways, customs and beliefs of the Garhwalis. Last, but certainly not the least, is Commander Jogindar Singh, whose special knowledge and experience in the Garhwal region and its potential for tourism has made him an acknowledged expert. His introduction is brief yet comprehensive.

Finally, I must thank the one to whom the book is dedicated, Sarah Shakuntla. Without her cooperation, good nature and high spirits in spite of almost being ignored by her parents, none of this would have been completed.

I would be happy to share more detailed information should anyone wish to contact me.

April 1986　　　　GURMEET THUKRAL
London House
Mussoorie.

Page 14 –
The temple
village of Ran
17 km above
Guptakashi
along the route
Madmaheshw
The temple is
significant bein
the site of a
perpetual yag
(fire and
worship) where
the fire is
constantly fuel
and prayers
are chanted
continuously. I
the foreground
villager plows
his fields in
the age-old
tradition.

Garhwal: A Perspective

NESTLING in the midst of the Himalaya is *Garhwal*—the abode of the gods, and of the eternal snows. It is a land of sages, religion and cults; of sacred rivers, holy confluences, alpine lakes, thundering waterfalls, and hot springs. A storehouse of myths and legends, it is a place of pilgrimages and spiritual fulfilments.

This divine wilderness is the trekker's delight, the mountaineer's challenge, the photographer's paradise, Nature's own botanical garden, and a sanctuary of variegated fauna.

Geographically, Garhwal lies between the latitudes 29°-26'-31°-28' N and longitudes 79°-49'-80°-6' E. The elevation profile begins with the foothills, the Shivaliks meeting the dun (600 m) on the south. The rolling dun gives way to the first ridges of the Lesser Himalaya. Higher still are the Mid Himalaya, and finally the relief rises dramatically to the Greater Himalaya, with its towering peaks covered with age-old snows, forming the Indo-Tibetan border, on the north. Kumaon lies to the east, and Himachal Pradesh to the west. The area covers the river catchments of the Ganga, the Yamuna, and the Nayar, their drainage pattern crisscrossing the region.

Garhwal was named during the fifteenth century, when King Ajai Pal began the unification of the principalities, finally forging the fifty-two *Garhs* (fortresses) into one kingdom. Ajai Pal shifted his capital from Chandpurgarhi to Joshimath, then to Dewalgarh. Finally, the capital of the Garhwal Raj was set up at Srinagar, to commemorate the completion of the unification.

The Gurkha invasion of Garhwal put the Garhwal Raj in debt. After the Gurkhas were defeated in the year 1815, with the help of the British, the King was forced to cede Pauri and Chamoli to them in payment. The capital of Garhwal or of what was left of it, was established at Tehri.

Long after the independence of India, the merger of Tehri Raj made way for the reconstitution of the five hill districts of Uttar Pradesh into the present Garhwal division.

Garhwal has a prehistory hidden beneath the heavy veils of time. Recent archaeological finds place the date of some settlements as 800 BC.

Garhwal was formerly known as Kedarkhand. It was here that Shiva was traditionally worshipped. There are also strong suggestions of Buddhism and Jainism; the *Siddh* and *Nath* cult and *Naga* worship have had their days here. Tantra too had a strong following in the region, but gradually lost ground with the consecration of the Badrinath temple in the ninth century AD, when Vishnu worship gained a foothold. It is generally accepted that Shankaracharya (AD 788-820), a Namboodri Brahmin from Kerala, the great social reformer, established the Vishnu image at Badrinath AD 815-20. He died at Kedarnath in AD 820, where his *samadhi* (final resting place) is located, a befitting memorial to one who revitalised the Hindu faith all over the country.

The *Vedas* (the books of knowledge of the Aryans), were composed in Garhwal (the best known to the Garhwalis being the *Atharvaveda*) and they make telltale references to various geographical features of this region. The practice of horoscopy and astrology, offshoots of Vedic knowledge, flourished, and Deoprayag remains an important

centre for the production of astrological charts and calenders.

The area of Badri-Kedar is also called *Devbhumi*, or the Land of the Gods. Scripture has it that Garhwal was the theatre for many an episode of the gods, their place of abode, their playground and their gateway to heaven. Garhwal is steeped in mythology so much so that every stone acquires a sanctity of its own. A temple presents itself at every bend of the road or trail;

Facing page— "Srinagar, old capital of the Ruler of Garhwal. The Gorakhnath Cave, the Sri Yantra, Kamleshwara Temple, Raj Rajeshwari Temple and the Alaknanda River are situated here." (Translated from the painting). This is an example of the Garhwal School of Miniature Painting by Jwala Ram c. 1890. Courtesy Garhwal University Museum.

The Alaknanda flows past the present-day Srinagar, and forms the divide between Tehri and Pauri districts. In spite of devastating floods which destroyed most of the Raja's Srinagar it has re-emerged as the educational center of Garhwal.

Views along the Panch Kedar trek, Chaukhambha Peaks and the fallen log bridge, crossing the Dudh Ganga.

Facing page—A typical view of terraced fields sculpted over generations, that have sustained Garhwal for centuries. In these fields are grown the staples of the Garhwali's diet: millet, wheat, barley, rice and seasonal vegetables.

each hilltop is a divine abode; and every river or stream is holy, because it is a part of and tributary to the sacrosanct Ganga.

There is still more to Garhwal, and it meets the eye! Its mountains and valleys, forests and meadows, birds, butterflies and flowers are all in perfect harmony—its sights, scents, sounds, and silence provide a sensual delight!

Hardwar, where the Ganga enters the plains, is the gateway to Garhwal. Other entry points are Kotdwar and Kalsi, where the Yamuna enters the plains. No matter what the route, one sees mighty rivers raging by.

Deoprayag, at the confluence of the Alaknanda and the Bhagirathi, where the Ganga (by name) begins, is the most important of the *panch prayags* (five holy confluences). The other four confluences, all on the Alaknanda, are Rudraprayag, Karanprayag, Nandprayag, and Vishnuprayag.

The Yamuna flows westerly in the region. Interesting places in its valley are Barawala, a *yagya* site of great antiquity; Kalsi, the site of a rock inscription of Ashoka; and, Lakhamandal, famous for its Pandava legends and folklore. Part of the Yamuna valley is known as Jaunsar. This pocket has its cultural peculiarities. The social anthropologists have highlighted only the practice of polyandry; there is much more of interest awaiting anyone who wishes to take a closer look into this unique region.

Yamunotri, the source of the Yamuna, is

one of the four *dhams* (pilgrims' major destination). A pilgrim to the four *dhams* has to visit them *vamvarta*, from the left to the right (west to east in this case), reaching Yamunotri, Gangotri, Kedarnath, and Badrinath, in that order. Accomplishing these four *dhams* is regarded to be a complete and final pilgrimage, ensuring *moksha* (salvation) for the devout pilgrim.

A more intensive pilgrimage for a Shaivite would be the *Panch Kedari* (five temples of Shiva), and that for a Vaishnava, the *Panch Badris* (five temples of Badri). Other ancient temples of Kedar are Gopeshwar (Go-sthal) in Chamoli district, Budh Kedar in Tehri district, and Binsar in Pauri district; while those of Badri are Adi-Badri, Chandpur Garh and Kalp Badri at Urgam.

Situated by a lake at 4,150 m are Hemkund Sahib, a prominent Sikh shrine, and Lakshman Siddh, a Hindu one. Roop Kund another high altitude lake, is intriguing on account of the human remains found there. According to popular legends, the skeletons and armour of a medieval army lies at the bottom. Sahastra Tal, Dodi Tal, Maser Tal, Pain Tal, Kedar Tal, Vasuki Tal, and Deoria Tal, all carry their own legends and are attractive destinations for the angler and the trekker.

Between the tree-line and the snow-line are lush alpine meadows, called *buggyals*. The spring and monsoon showers awaken a profusion of flowers of various sizes, hues, shapes, and fragrances, which greet each weary step of the traveller to the *buggyals*. The Valley of Flowers is one of them, and is well known. Har-ki-dun, another floral valley, also has its visitors. But there are numerous, nameless valleys where many a flower has blossomed and withered unseen. The rare Himalayan yellow lotus, called *Brahamkamal* is the most important flower of the region, as it is used as ritual offering.

Higher up are the eternal snows, the towering Nanda Devi, Shivling, Trisul, Kamet, Kedarnath, and the glaciers which are holy to the Hindu.

The mountaintop lakes mirror the icy ruggedness of the lofty peaks.

The *Khos* and the *Kiratas* are thought to be the original inhabitants of Garhwal. Relics of the animistic faith of such a people are still visible in the form of the local deity of each settlement, as also in certain rituals peculiar to some places.

Gradually various immigrants settled in Garhwal, bringing their own faith and rituals.

Waves of migrations are said to have taken place during the Sultanate, with the motive of escaping religious persecution, preserving their deities, prestige, and life. The new settlers must have interacted with the natives in a very complex manner, as it is virtually impossible to distinguish the one from the other today. However, in many a case, the name the new settlers gave to their village has a ring of where they came from. There are places with names like Nagpur, Ajmer, Rampur, Udaipur, Joshiana, and Gujarara, that have deep echoes of associations.

Ironically, in the land of the *Vedas*, society is classified into three castes, as against the usual four. They are Brahmins, the Rajputs, (Kshatriyas), and the Doms (Shudras). The *Vaishyas*, the trader of the four-fold division, probably was not needed in the hilly, agrarian set-up. Whatever trade there was in Garhwal was in the hands of the *Bhotias* (the Marchas and the Jads), a tribal group with its own culture having affinities with Tibetans. This fossilised three-tier system has come to stay in Garhwal—a Vedic anomaly.

Garhwal has been and still is an agrarian society, eking out a living from the staircase fields. With the population going up, subsistence agriculture could hardly support the mounting pressure for food. Nor was there ever work for many. Obviously an out-migration would result, as it did.

Recruitment during the British regime in India, especially during the nineteenth century took a large number of Garhwalis into the

A waterfall among thousands, this one is at Atri Muni Guffa (cave) above Mandal.

army, a vocation that is still a big draw with them. Less lucky ones went to the plains as domestic servants. At the same time, many individual Garhwalis have done rather well with many holding high offices in pre-and post-partition India.

One result of out-migration has been the institution of what is popularly called "money order economy" of Garhwal. Another is that though the set-up is patriarchal, the woman is now the backbone of the society. She is

Above – Villagers traditionally dress in home-spun woollen garments. Children of both sexes don ornaments at an early age. A hooka (water smoking pipe) is a universal appliance in Garhwali homes.

Facing page – Lord Ganesh, the remover of obstacles, is the first of the Hindu gods to be prayed to especially at the start of any new venture. Brahamkamal, flower exclusive to the Himalaya is given as ritual offering. This idol is located at Khelu Binayak at the start of the treacherous lap of the Nanda Raj Jat (Roop-Kund-Homkund).
Along any route, villagers are both willing and unwilling to be photographed. No matter how poor, a woman never goes unadorned. Village houses are mud and stone constructions with slate roofs, and generally vegetables growing above.

responsible for the domestic chores, as well as for crop production, save for the tilling of the soil.

The dress of the highlander is homespun woollen wear. The traditional dress consists of upper and lower garments. The cut and style of the garments of the plains are missing. Usually a blanket is wrapped around the upper body and pinned with an iron pin fashioned by the local blacksmith. Men will add pants and women a skirt with additional shirts and sweaters depending on the altitude of the wearer. Goathair is used for making *dhokas*, waterproof outer garments of the shepherd. Strong ropes too are made of goathairs. In Jaunpur and Jaunsar, knitted shoes and matting is made of goathair. Here the dress is colourful and consists of a blouse and a skirt that is of ankle length. Men wear a shirt and pajamas with a waist-coat. Especially during festivals, the women are striking in their richly embroidered and bejewelled apparel.

In the warmer valleys, cotton dresses are worn. The common dress today is a saree and blouse for women, and a shirt and pants for men. Gaudy colours—Indian pink, bright yellow, loud blues, greens and red—are popular with women, adding colour to an otherwise drab life.

Jewellery is another attractive feature in Garhwal. In some areas, traditionally, only the Brahmins and Rajputs wore gold, every-one else wore silver. In other areas this was not prevalent and all the castes wore

23

either. Thick *hanslis* (neck-bands), *dhagulas* (bracelets), and *paunta* (anklets) of chiseled silver are common to the region. Then there are gold ear-rings and auxiliary ear-rings; the *phulli* (nose-pin), worn on the side of the nose; and the *bulak* (nose-ring) that dangles awkwardly down the middle of the nose crossing the lips. The last mentioned has to be held aside during eating. There is also the exquisitely crafted, intricate, over-sized nose-ring (*nath*) for the bride. And there are the rings and the collar (*Gulband*). Silver coins of British India too were assembled into necklaces, buttons, and rings.

Although some items of jewellery have a common design throughout the region, others are distinctive to some areas. At a glance the wearer can be recognised as belonging to a particular area based on the design of an item of jewellery.

Garhwal has many attractions: its mountains, its mythology, its flora and fauna, its rivers and valleys, its villages and people. Each ridge, each turning of the path offers a new and exciting experience. Many motor roads have now been built to carry pilgrims and tourists from one vista to another, but the best way to explore Garhwal is by foot, climbing and descending the steep Himalaya over trails that wind their way through fields and forests. Nowhere in the world is there such a profusion of Nature in all its guises, so varied and so complete.

Facing page—The Ansuya Devi Temple located above Mandal is the site where couples seeking children come to propitiate the goddess Ansuya who if pleased will grant them the boon of offspring. Located behind the temple is a tree where a massive rock hurled by Bhima lies in the fork.

The Kalimath Temple 6 km from Guptakashi is the site of a large Bhagwati temple. Festivals are held annually with pilgrims travelling from throughout the country to be here. Ritual sacrifices are still commonly practised here.

Gateway to Uttrakhand

Hardwar

AS the name suggests, Hardwar (or Hari-dwar, Har—meaning Shiva, Hari—meaning Vishnu and dwar—meaning gate) is the passageway to the land of the gods. Pilgrimages to the four hill shrines traditionally start where the Ganga enters the plains. Mythology in India stems from a wooded retreat near Hardwar called *Kankhal*. Here the ancient Daksha Prajapati disturbed Lord Shiva from his yogic meditation in the deep Himalaya. Here too the gods brought the pitcher of nectar to foil the demons and this triumph is commemorated by the **Kumbh Mela** every twelfth year. Hindus revere the Ganga most at Har-ki-Pairi and the evening worship of the river goddess in her small temple in midstream is one of the most beautiful sights in India. Devotees light small lamps, nestling in flower-laden leaf boats, and send them downstream in the tugging current at sunset. The river follows a remarkable canal engineered by an Englishman, but such was his concern that the holiness of the river should be respected, that he placed a small hole in the dam diverting the Ganga so that it would always flow freely, and built 103 bathing ghats. In turn the Ganga canal has been accepted as the mainstream.

The bazaar alongside the river is full of atmosphere and the best time to visit it is during the month of Sravan (in the monsoon) when devotees come from hundreds of miles away to carry home pots of Ganga water on a yoke over their shoulders. They decorate the yoke with coloured silk flags and march in their thousands along the road to their villages; for some of them a week's walking marathon. Such is their devotion they return each year to turn the town into a magical feast of colour.

People arrive daily from all parts of India, and sometimes abroad, to immerse the family ashes in the river. The water changes colour according to the season. Often it takes on a brilliant blue, and the white waves caused by its breakneck speed add to the lovely spectacle. Bathers cling to chains to prevent being swept away and it seems certain this tremendous bore of water could easily wash away sins! In the monsoons the river turns green-brown as the glacial moraine of melting snows and the soil of many tributaries add to the flow.

Rishikesh

Hardwar has hundreds of temples which rise up on either side of the river as she bursts through the Shivalik range. On the way to Rishikesh through the 25 kilometer belt of

forest, the temples of Hardwar begin to be replaced by the ashrams of Rishikesh. Famous names like Swami Shivananda and Maharishi Mahesh run their ashrams alongside the Ganga on the northern fringe of the Shivaliks where the Ganga descends majestically from the Himalaya. Rishikesh is the ancient road-head for all pilgrim traffic and this small town in the season is hectic with groups of villagers from all over India clamouring for seats on the buses to the four hill shrines. The northern part of the town is called Muni-ki-Reti and refers to the silver shores of the river where the rishis of old meditated. Across the Ganga, large, sprawling but well-maintained ashrams teach yoga and publish books on the scriptures. A ferry will take you over, and a walk along the other bank for two kilometers, will bring you to the famous Lakshman Jhula bridge, which joins the main Badrinath road. Here are more temples and museums, for Rishikesh is essentially a pilgrim town, and the bulk of the pilgrims are simple villagers whose intense devotion give both Hardwar and Rishikesh a special atmosphere, a taste of the old India that continues to flow in modern dress as the Ganga canal has been harnessed to irrigate the fields of modern India. The grace of the goddess is what brings people to Hardwar in thanksgiving, and the visitor finds it hard to decide which is the more memorable, the beauty of the rushing waters or the beatific expression of the devotees.

Preceding page—Har-ki-Pairi, the most sacred bathing ghat in Hardwar, site of the Kumbh Mela, (which occurs in Hardwar every 12 years), when thousands of sadhus and hundreds of thousands of devotees ritually bathe in the Ganga to insure salvation.

Two sadhus on the banks of the Ganga at Rishikesh. In the background the portals of the Swarag Ashram, one of many.

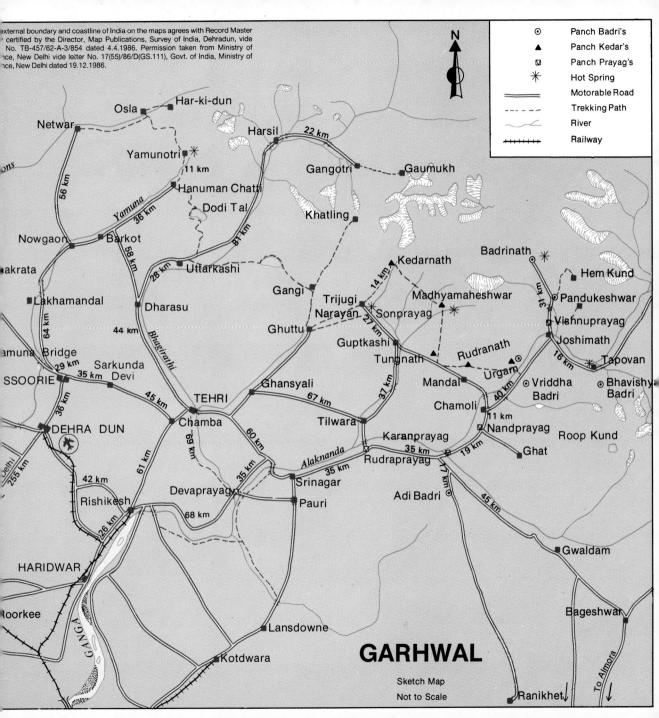

N

Panch Badri's
Panch Kedar's
Panch Prayag's
Hot Spring
Motorable Road
Trekking Path
River
Railway

Har-ki-dun
Osla
Netwar
Yamunotri
56 km
11 km
Hanuman Chatti
Yamuna
36 km
Dodi Tal
Nowgaon
Barkot
58 km
akrata
Lakhamandal
28 km
Uttarkashi
81 km
Dharasu
64 km
44 km
Bhagirathi
amuna Bridge
29 km
Sarkunda
Devi
SSOORIE
35 km
45 km
36 km
DEHRA DUN
61 km
69 km
42 km
Rishikesh
60 km
26 km
35 km
68 km
HARIDWAR
Roorkee
GANGA
Lansdowne
Kotdwara

Harsil
22 km
Gangotri
Gaumukh
Khatling
Gangi
Trijugi
Narayan
Sonprayag
Ghuttu
Guptkashi
27 km
Ghansyali
67 km
TEHRI
Chamba
Tilwara
37 km
Tungnath
Mandal
Chamoli
Karanprayag
35 km
19 km
Alaknanda
Rudraprayag
35 km
Srinagar
Pauri
Adi Badri
45 km
Devaprayag
Kedarnath
14 km
Madhyamaheshwar
Badrinath
Hem Kund
Pandukeshwar
Vishnuprayag
Joshimath
16 km
Tapovan
Rudranath
Urgam
40 km
Vriddha
Badri
Bhavishy
Badri
11 km
Nandprayag
Roop Kund
Ghat
Gwaldam
Bageshwar

GARHWAL

Sketch Map

Not to Scale

Ranikhet

To Almora

Two views of Deoprayag. "The Raghunath Temple established by the Shankaracharya stands at the confluence of the Bhagirathi and Alaknanda. This site is important and famous for Ram Brahmins." Courtesy— Garhwal University Museum.

The Panch
Prayags

Cradle of the Ganga

A MONGST the most sacred places on the pilgrimage to Badrinath are the five confluences of the seven rivers (they are the Vishnu Ganga, the Alaknanda, the Dhauli Ganga, the Nandakini, the Pinder, the Mandakini, the Bhagirathi, and the Nayar, which joins below Deoprayag) that form the Ganga. The holiest of these Prayags, Deoprayag, lies 70 km upstream from Rishikesh. Sometimes written as Devprayag, this dramatic meeting place of the Bhagirathi and Alaknanda rivers is actually the point where the name Ganga is first used for the most loved river of India. The ancient village nestles between the furious torrents and the motor road. The massive and shapely temple of Raghunath indicates a Vaishnava influence and the Pandas (priests) of Deoprayag do in fact officiate at Badrinath. This must be one of the most fascinating villages of India, visited by millions of Hindus over the ages. The population is predominately Brahmins coming from South India. This was the entry to all the four sacred shrines of Uttrakhand. The Pandas here acted as guides helping the pilgrims accomplish their yatra. The pilgrims climbed from the Alaknanda and crossed the watershed to descend to the Bhagirathi at Tehri. Thence they proceeded westwards to the source of the Yamuna and retraced their steps east to culminate at Badri.

The word *prayag* refers to an auspicious place for sacrifice and the most important prayag is at the confluence of the Ganga and the Yamuna at Allahabad. The ancient name for this Allahabad *sangam* (meeting place) is still referred to as Prayag Raj. Upstream of Deoprayag on the Alaknanda lie the other four prayags. Rudraprayag is famous as the junction for the Badrinath and Kedarnath roads. Here at the small temple dedicated to Rudra, the ancient fiery, roaring aspect of Lord Shiva, the green waters between of the Mandakini meet the glacial flood of the Alaknanda. In the small bazaar stands an enormous banyan tree and most pilgrims stop here to rest awhile and eat at the wayside restaurants. Rudraprayag is also famous as the home of the world's most deadly man-eater which in the 1920s accounted for some 300 victims. It was finally shot by the great shikari Jim Corbett in 1926. A commemorative stone marks the spot a few kilometers south of the bazaar.

The third prayag is the union of the Pinder with the Alaknanda at Karanprayag. Not a particularly scenic spot, this is an important and topographical junction in the area. Along the Pinder lies the route to the neighbouring province of Kumaon which has always been a traditional rival to Garhwal. The original capital of Garhwal guards its frontier at Chandpurgarhi. Here the great Himalaya start and the towering ramparts take over from the verdant lesser ranges. Above Karanprayag with its association with

Kakar Phali, (where the deer can jump), where the mighty Alaknanda, 6 km upstream of Rudraprayag narrows through this gorge. There is Pandava legend that Shiva, who was being pursued by the Pandavas, entered the rock below by the river and emerged above. Even now, when fires are lit, the smoke travels along the same route. A temple is located below next to the river.

the heroes of the Mahabharata epic, stands the small confluence of Nandprayag, said to be the area in which the Sanskrit dramatist, Kalidas sited the famous love story Shakuntala. As with many of these sites on the bank of the Alaknanda, the original temples have been washed away by a series of devastating floods over the years. Nand was the father of Lord Krishna, while Nanda was the daughter of the snows. The most revered mountain of Uttrakhand, Nanda Devi rises above the source of the Nandakini which meets the Alaknanda at Nandprayag. In modern times this was the spot, Hillary's Sea to Sky jetboat expedition could reach, before being defeated by the whitewater.

The fifth of the prayags lies at Vishnu-prayag, marked only by a temple, for the steep walls of the Dhauli Ganga canyon allow no room for a village. Here the Alaknanda turns north for the final stretch between the sheer cliffs to the goal at Badrinath. Some sadhus hold that this dangerous confluence demands an annual human sacrifice and that the river wears a sinister aspect until a pilgrim is offered in appeasement. These old pilgrim routes have their own cautionary tales and it should be remembered that in the olden days many aged devotees considered these holy confluences to be the most auspicious place to meet their gods. Hence the tangible reverence attached to these five prayags.

The temple at Kharsali with a leopard perched atop, a symbol of the cult. The structure hails from a period of strong Buddhist influence (note the stupa-like formation on the left).

The Yamuna Valley

Yamunotri

THE waters of the Yamuna have seen India's history unfold. The Yamuna has continued flowing while many empires were created, flourished and fell in ruin. The most recent of these, the Mughals, left the largest mark on her shores, from Delhi's Red Fort, to the Taj Mahal. The source of the second holiest river is close to Mother Ganga. The frozen waters of Saptarishi Kund at the base of Kalinda Parbat are sole witness to Yamuna's birth (the area is very inaccessible). She joins the Ganga and Saraswati (which is believed to flow underground) at Allahabad (Prayag Raj) after kilometers of wandering through the plains.

Yamuna is said to be fickle-minded. If the course of her river is an indication, then this may very well be true. She meanders sluggishly about in startling contrast to the full-bodied raging river that she is at her beginning.

Yamuna is the twin sister of Yama, the Lord of Death. It is believed that those who bathe in her waters will be spared a tortuous death. Yama will look kindly upon them. Yamuna is also the daughter of Surya, the sun, and Sangya, meaning consciousness. Sangya was unable to keep her eyes open in Surya's presence and when she did open them she was unable to gaze directly at him. Surya noticed this and commented that she would certainly have a fickle-minded daughter.

Yamuna is so fickle that every few years her temple at Yamunotri (3,291 m) must be rebuilt. During the winter, snow, and in the spring, floods, seem to ensure that Yamuna has a new temple every few years.

Near the temple are three hot springs; the higher, Surya Kund, is the most important. Into it are placed rice and potatoes tied in a handkerchief to be cooked in its boiling water and later taken home as "prasad".

The Pandas of Yamunotri are from the village of Kharsali, 6 km below Yamunotri. Here, the temple is said to have reached 15 stories high. It is presently only three stories high and presumably has been rebuilt since its glorious days. The original structure may hail from the time of strong Buddhist influence. Atop the temple is a leopard statue. The view from the top of the temple is of the Yamunotri peaks to the north-east.

Yamunotri Trek

From Har-ki-dun there is a route over a ridge to Yamunotri. It is a steep ascent and then a steep descent of 29 km reaching Yamunotri above the temple on the left

A view of the Yamunotri temple complex. The Yamuna forms from three tributaries.

Facing page—Bandar Punch (Monkey's Tail) from Aineha Pass along the Yamunotri-Dodi Tal-Uttarkashi trek.

side. The snow comes early here and melts late in the spring so the best time to do this is during the summer or early fall.

The trek to Yamunotri begins from Hanumanchatti. To Phulchatti it is a 7 km gradual ascent and a further 3 km is Jankichatti. Another route to Jankichatti is via the temple village of Kharsoli, the home of the pandas of the Yamunotri Temple. It is only another 1 km and is a must. After Jankichatti the climb is steep to Yamunotri but it is only 5 km.

Behind the temple is the route to Saptarishi Kund, the source of the Yamuna. Follow along the left side of the Yamuna but not along the trail up the ridge to Har-ki-dun. It is *not* a clear path but it is worth a try. Stay along the left until after the waterfall then turn toward the right.

Dodi Tal

After visiting Yamunotri, a route can be taken to Gangotri, part trek and part bus. Enroute, Dodi Tal, one of the loveliest lakes in Garhwal, lies at an altitude of 3,024 m. A forest bungalow built on the shores provides relative comfort while the trout in the lake provides meals as sumptuous as any in the world's best restaurants. Of course, one's appetite is heightened by both the altitude and the 30 km hike from Hanumanchatti or the 38 km hike from Gangori (5 km from Uttarkashi). The lake setting could not have been better chosen. Deodar and pine act as guardians for the numerous

wild flowers. Above Dodi Tal is a ridge (one crosses this on the route from Yamunotri) where there are the views of the snows. Going up the left hand side of the stream offers the best view of Bandar Punch.

The area around Dodi Tal is still fairly wild and a variety of wild life can be seen coming to the lake shores early morning and late evenings for water. A road is proposed that will reach Dodi Tal shores.

Dodi Tal Trek

The trek for Dodi Tal generally begins from Gangori 5 km above Uttarkashi (take a bus or truck going to Gangotri). To Kalyani it is possible to catch a truck, during good weather this is a motorable road. From here to Agoda it is 5 km steep ascent. Dodi Tal is a further 16 km steep ascent.

Above Dodi Tal is a ridge with an excellent

view of Bandar Punch. It is possible to take a day trek or continue to Yamunotri.

From Hanumanchatti follow the Hanuman Ganga along the right. A village lies 4 km along and from here a further 3 km are some houses where potatoes are grown. Try to keep along the ridge as closely as possible on the right away from the river Aineha Pass is at the top of the ridge and Dodi Tal lies 6 km below along a steep descent. Several log bridges must be crossed along the way.

Har-Ki-Dun

Another name for Uttrakhand was Panchaldesh (land of the five) referring to the Panch Pandava brothers. They figure in the entire Garhwal but especially in the Jaunsar-Fateh Parvat region where the villagers actually claim to be descended from the Pandavas and their arch rivals the Kauravas.

Hari-ki-dun, a relatively small, unspoilt valley very similar to the Valley of the Flowers, is 8 km from Osla the last village in the region. To some trekkers it is a preferable destination as it involves more of

Facing page—Dodi Tal, often described as an anglers' paradise. On the far shore are log huts constructed by the forestry department.

Wild flowers abound throughout Garhwal, untouched and unspoiled by man.

Upper right—Inula Grandiflora
Lower Right—Morina Longifolia

Typical Alpine homes in the Fateh Parvat region. The village of Naitwar pictured here is representative of the intricately carve wooden structures decorating both homes and temples.

Facing page – Mother and Child

Page 43 – The Peak Swargarohini, also known by its translated name, the pathway to heaven. It is one of a number of named and un-named peaks in the region. Har-ki-dun is another valley where many flowers are found.

a trek, is not so often visited, and is not yet commercialised. From Har-ki-dun it is possible to climb many named and un-named peaks and to cross over the ridge to Yamunotri.

Of the named peaks, Swargarohini is of special interest. The main summit, 6,252 m, is still unclimbed by modern day mountaineers. *Modern day* is mentioned because according to legend, the Pandavas, Draupadi (their common wife) and their dog climbed the mountain when they left the earth. Swargarohini means "The Path to Heaven".

The source of the Har-ki-dun Gad (a tributary of the Tons) lies at the back of the valley at the Jamdar glacier. Those who have trekked through the area claim that it is the best pine and deodar forest in all of Asia. Of course, like many of the valleys in the Garhwal area the best time to visit and see the multitude of flowers blooming is during the monsoons.

Har-ki-dun lies in the region known as Fateh-Parvat. It has been very isolated and modernisation has come very slowly and painfully. The people here share their cultural heritage with the Jaunsaris. They practice polyandry (and to some extent polygamy) because their ancestors, the Pandava brothers, shared one wife, but also as an economic necessity both to keep the population down and to prevent the division of property. The women are bought and sold like commodities and their value goes up after a child is born, and after a divorce. The system of bride-price and the expense of weddings has led to many problems.

As in most areas in Garhwal the woman is the backbone of the family. She carries the day's water supply to the home, gathers wood, cooks, plants, weeds, harvests the fields, and cares for the livestock and the children. Men plow the fields (but only if animals i.e. buffalo or ox, are used in the fields; when the plowing must be done by hand the woman does this also), and some spin wool. Unfortunately the woman's position does not reflect the life-sustaining work that she does. She is first the victim of her father and later her husband. She believes in the archaic saying "pati devta swaroop" (husband is God).

The beliefs of the locals are very interesting. At Naitwar, a Mahasudevta temple is particularly beautiful with its intricate carvings. There is a legend behind the Mahasudevta (also spelled deota). A man was ploughing his fields when a snake arose before him and told him to worship his image (Mahasudevta) here and it would reveal the laws that are to be obeyed. At Taluka, a temple is dedicated to Duryodhana, the eldest Kaurava brother, who fought the Pandavas in many battles. Also King Bhogdutta, who

supported the Kauravas in the fateful battle of Kurukshetra, has a temple dedicated to him.

Interesting methods of worship occur in Fateh-Parvat. In Pakola the idol is worshipped with the back facing the worshippers. The worship of Duryodhana is done by throwing shoes upon the idol.

After leaving the Fateh-Parvat region, one enters the Jaunsar region. Jaunsar-Bawar lies

41

along the Yamuna valley. Sculptures found in and around the Lakhamandal area show a strong Greco-Roman influence and many believe that the people of both these areas are descendants of Kushan and Hun invaders. The seat of the empire was near Kalsi and the culture has been preserved close to its original form in the Jaunsar-Fateh-Parvat region due to its inaccessibility.

Har-Ki-Dun Trek

The roadhead to Har-Ki-Dun is at Naitwar. From here a 12 km gradual ascent is Saur. From here to Taluka is 11 km also a gradual ascent. Near Osla is a Forest Rest House, 11 km again along a gradual ascent. The village of Osla is across the river but it is well worth the trip to visit the intricately carved wooden temple. From this Forest Rest House to the one at Har-ki-Dun it is 8 km of steep climbing. Further up the Ruinsara Gad is a lake and one of the base camps for climbing Swargarohini. Following the Maninder Gad leads to other sites for base camps for many nearby peaks.

Lakhamandal

The Lakhamandal village is typical of Jaunsar. It is easily reached by crossing a rope bridge at Kuan above Kalsi. The temple here is another famous location of Pandava fame. Lakhamandal gets its name from a story of intrigue.

After their defeat in the epic war, re-told in the Mahabharata, the Kauravas sought to avenge themselves by destroying the Pandavas. A huge structure, Lakhamandir, (of lac) was constructed for the Pandavas' stay when they reached the site. After the Pandavas were inside, the shellac was set ablaze. The Pandavas, however, had discovered the plot and arranged to have a tunnel dug through which they made their escape.

The Pandavas dance, a peculiar feature of Jaunsar, re-enacts many episodes from the life of the Pandavas.

The Madhu Mahadev temple here dates back to the 8th century AD. The present day Lakhamandal has re-occupied an area that was once a great civilisation. Ploughing the fields continues to yield stone images of the Hindu pantheon. The temple is a protected monument and holds numerous sculptures dating from the same time. Shiva-lingas have

been found by the hundreds.

Fairs and festivals form an integral part of an otherwise dull life. They celebrate the Hindu festivals but have several unique ones of their own. "Maun" is a summer-time celebration centered around fishing. A potent plant is dried and powdered and then thrown into the river to stun the fish which are then easily caught. While the men are occupied, the women take the opportunity to talk, relax and show off their jewellery. "Pancho", celebrated in May, is the time when the Mahasudevta idol is taken out of the temple and bathed. In August "Jagra" festival centres around Mahasudevta when the idol is taken out in a procession.

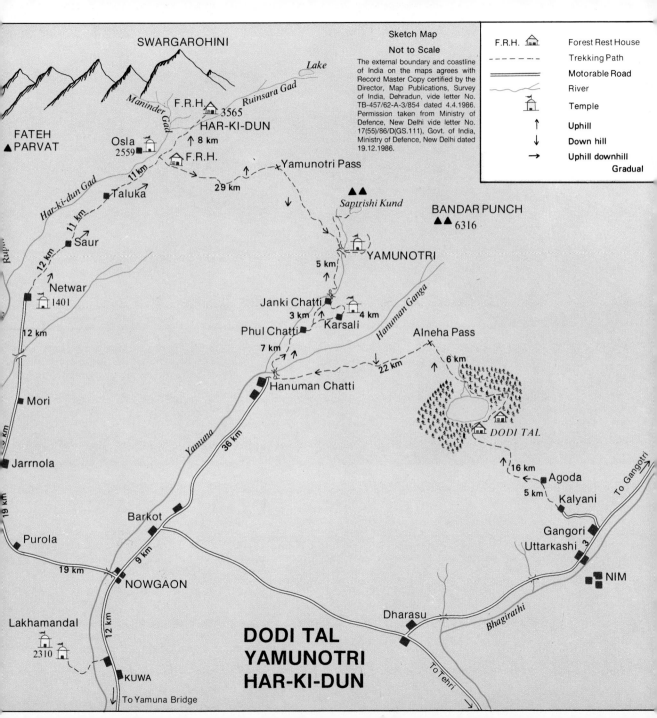

SWARGAROHINI

FATEH
PARVAT

Maninder Gad

F.R.H.
3565
HAR-KI-DUN

Lake
Ruinsara Gad

Osla
2559

↑ 8 km

F.R.H.

Har-ki-dun Gad

11 km

Taluka

29 km

Yamunotri Pass

↓

Saptrishi Kund

BANDAR PUNCH
6316

11 km

Saur

12 km

↑

Netwar
1401

↓ 5 km

YAMUNOTRI

↑

12 km

↕

Mori

Janki Chatti

3 km ↑ ↑

Karsali

4 km

Phul Chatti

Hanuman Ganga

Alneha Pass

7 km ↑ ↑

↓ 22 km

6 km ↑

Yamuna

36 km

Hanuman Chatti

DODI TAL

Jarrnola

16 km

Agoda

To Gangotri

5 km

Kalyani

Barkot

9 km

Gangori

Purola

19 km

Uttarkashi

3

NIM

19 km

NOWGAON

Dharasu

Bhagirathi

Lakhamandal
2310

12 km

KUWA

↓ To Yamuna Bridge

To Tehri

DODI TAL
YAMUNOTRI
HAR-KI-DUN

F.R.H.	Forest Rest House
	Trekking Path
	Motorable Road
	River
	Temple
↑	Uphill
↓	Down hill
→	Uphill downhill
	Gradual

Gangotri settlement. The temple is located in the left center. Gangotri was the most inaccessible of the four dhams. Now a motorable road leads almost to the temple doors with only intermittent breaks from landslides.

Facing page—Gaurikund, referred to as the most beautiful falls in Garhwal, certainly by merit of the rock sculpturing done by the hands of Mother Ganga.

Gangotri: The Source

GANGOTRI—source of India's holiest river, refuge of rishis and sages escaping the evils of the world, and 'goal' of road weary pilgrims seeking salvation. Gangotri, at the time of the Vedas, was the actual source of the Ganga, now it is the representative site. The glacial source has receded a further 19 km to Gaumukh. Gangotri means "Ganga flowing north" because at the time of its emergence from the glacier at the base of the Bhagirathi peaks it does flow northwards. Gaumukh means cow's snout,

and for the imaginative, the wide expanse at the end of the glacier where the Ganga emerges, already a raging torrential river, there is a resemblance.

The legend re-told in "The Legends of India's Rivers" by Manoj Dass, about the creation of Ganga, is an enchanting tale. Narada, a sage, who had free access to the Himalaya, Land of the Gods, enjoyed singing and playing his Veena while he walked through the area. One day he happened upon a group of very beautiful people whom he could not identify (he knew all the gods and goddesses). He asked them who they were and learned that they were the Souls of the Ragas and Raginis. They were all mutilated in some way or the other, missing some part of their body, a hand, a limb, or

an eye. When asked how they came to be so injured, they hesitantly replied that those people like Narada who sang and played their music so badly and carelessly caused their mutilation. Narada, horrified by what he had done, asked how he could help them. He was told that Shiva, the best singer, should be asked to sing and then they would be healed. Narada hastened to Shiva who

Pilgrims, pandas, and sadhus journey to Gangotri, the honoured source of Ganga where puja is performed by all.

Above—The devotees are at Gaumukh where the Ganga re-emerges from under the glacier. Above the glacier several streams join and flow under the glacier. The upper reaches of Garhwal have been the traditional retreat of ascetics, rishis and sadhus.

agreed to sing if perfect listeners could be found. The perfect listeners, Vishnu and Brahma, agreed immediately because Shiva sang very infrequently. Soon after Shiva began singing, the Ragas and Raginis were healed and made whole. While Shiva sang Vishnu identified with the music so completely that he began to flow like water. Brahma quickly used his *Kamandalu* to contain the water, Ganga, as it was then called. This was how Ganga was created and why Ganga water is considered holy. It is the divine body in liquid form.

After Ganga's creation another event brought her to earth. Brahma allowed the Ganga to flow because of the pious devotion of the sage Bhagiratha who meditated at Gangotri. Bhagiratha desired the Ganga to restore his ancestors who had been turned to ash. She flowed to earth over the tangled locks of Shiva's hair, because the earth could not bear the full force of the Ganga descending.

Many question Gangotri as the true source, claiming that the Alaknanda flowing from Badrinath is the larger source of the Ganga. However, when Shiva broke Ganga's fall his hair dispersed the water throughout Uttrakhand also called the cradle of the Ganga. All rivers and streams in this area have some association with Ganga and add Ganga to their names. Gangotri is the honoured source of Mother Ganga because not only did Bhagiratha meditate here but it was here that Ganga first touched earth.

The small settlement of Gangotri is a seasonal attraction as are the other *dhams*. The temple was built from stone carried from a location 20 km away, and is over 250 years old, erected by Aman Singh Thapa, a Gurkha commander.

With the coming of winter snow and cold all, but the hardiest of sadhus, retreat to the relative warmth of areas downstream.

The road now forges an accessible route to Gangotri. The population has grown, meeting the needs of the growing number of pilgrims. An unfortunate aspect of modern rapid transport by bus, jeep, car and taxi, has been the loss of revenue to the Pandas. Throughout Garhwal, these religion-oriented tour guides have fallen into hard times. The total time spent by the pilgrim at the dham has decreased. Pilgrims were the Pandas mainstay. These

Enroute to Gaumukh is Chir Bhasa (abode of the pines) where the view is of Bhagirathi peaks III and I.

Upper left—Bhagirathi II and unnamed peak.
Middle left—Kedar Dome.
Lower left—Vasuki peak with Vasuki Tal below.
Above and Facing page—Shivling is the object of devotion
for Shiva devotees. At dawn water is offered to Shivling.

52

ill-fated men need the pilgrims far more than the pilgrims need them. Gone are the days when pilgrims would spend days resting for their onward journey, gone also is the need for experienced help through the variable countryside to the next dham. It is no wonder that the Pandas leap upon pilgrims as a tiger or a leopard would leap upon an unwary young deer.

Many say that Gangotri has changed. With the passing of the pandas and their system of chattis a new class of board and lodging has arisen. Some call themselves hotels and some "ashrams" in the hope of luring unsuspecting pilgrims. A few sadhus and munis uphold the age-old tradition of ashrams, expecting nothing in return.

From Gangotri many treks can be taken and more alluring to some, many mountains can be climbed. Interestingly, to reach Gango-

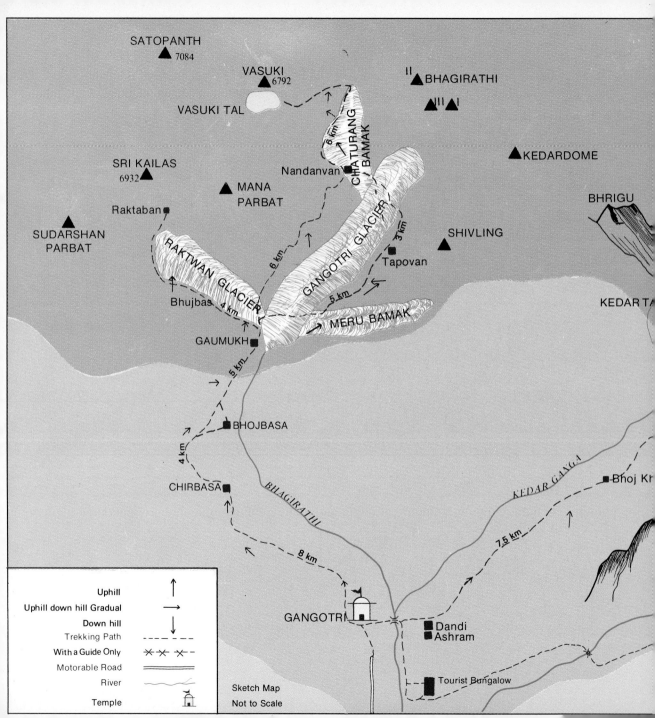

GANGOTRI REGION

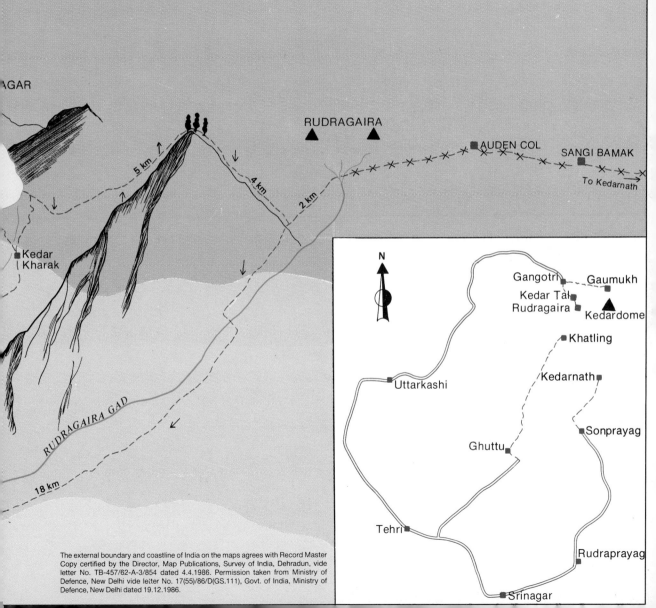

RUDRAGAIRA

AUDEN COL

SANGI BAMAK

To Kedarnath

5 km

4 km

2 km

Kedar
Kharak

RUDRAGAIRA GAD

18 km

N

Gangotri   Gaumukh
Kedar Tal
Rudragaira   Kedardome

Khatling

Kedarnath

Uttarkashi

Sonprayag

Ghuttu

Tehri

Rudraprayag

Srinagar

The external boundary and coastline of India on the maps agrees with Record Master
Copy certified by the Director, Map Publications, Survey of India, Dehradun, vide
letter No. TB-457/62-A-3/854 dated 4.4.1986. Permission taken from Ministry of
Defence, New Delhi vide letter No. 17(55)/86/D(GS.111), Govt. of India, Ministry of
Defence, New Delhi dated 19.12.1986.

tri one actually crosses through the Greater Himalaya. Many of the major peaks lie in a southward direction, especially from Gaumukh. Among the nearby peaks are Shivling (6,543 m), Sudarshan Parvat (6,507 m), Bhagirathi peaks, I (6,856 m), II (6,512 m), III (6,454 m), Srikailash (6,932 m) and Vasuki Parvat (6,792 m).

The Rudragaira peaks east of Gangotri are the training camps for the Nehru Institute of Mountaineering. For pilgrims, trekkers or mountaineers, Gangotri is the source.

Treks in Gangotri Region

Options:

1. Gangotri-Rudragaira-Khatling-Kedarnath
2. Gangotri-Kedar Tal-Rudragaira
3. Gangotri-Gaumukh-Tapovan
4. Gangotri-Gaumukh-Nandanvan-Vasuki-Tal
5. Gangotri-Gaumukh-Tapovan-Nandanvan
6. Gangotri-Gaumukh-Bhoj Bhasa-Raktaban

Gangotri-Gaumukh

Gangotri to Chir Basa is 6 km gradual ascent followed by a 2 km steep ascent. From here to Bhoj Bhasa is a 4 km gradual ascent. Bhoj Bhasa to Gaumukh is fairly flat and straight.

Gaumukh-Tapovan is 5 km. After crossing the glacier it is a 2 km steep ascent then 3 km gradual ascent.

Tapovan-Nandavan is 3 km crossing the glacier.

Nandavan-Vasuki Tal is a 6 km steep ascent.

Nandanvan-Gaumukh is a very steep rocky 6 km descent. It is easier to cross back to Tapovan and descend that way.

Kedar Tal

Born of the melt of the Thalesagar snows is Kedar Tal, a large emerald lake, at an altitude of 5,000 m. It lies between the Bhrigu peak and the Rudragaira group of mountains, approximately 17 km from Gangotri.

The overflow of the Kedar Tal gushes

Facing page—Kedar Tal and the glacier at the base of the Thalesagar Peak which is the source of the Kedar Ganga.

Bhoj Kharak (Birch grove) where the birch end enroute to Kedar Tal.

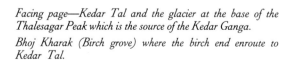

Above—The ridge dividing the Kedar Ganga river bed and the Rudragaira Gad. These rock piles act both as markers directing the trekker to the pass and as testimony to those who have passed previously (tradition dictates that a rock be added when the trekker reaches this point).

Below—Bharal, indigenous to this area, graze freely along the ridges and in the buggyals undisturbed by man.

Right—Rudragaira peaks are often used as training peaks for the Nehru Institute of Mountaineering based in Uttarkashi. From here a high altitude route crosses via Khatling.

through rocky glacial terrain, flows through the relatively flat meadow, Kedar Kharak, then rushes another 12 km, in its eager haste to meet the Bhagirathi at Gangotri.

Coming from the direction of Kedarnath, the Kedar Ganga is considered Lord Shiva's contribution to the Bhagirathi. It is the first tributary to the Bhagirathi; the second, the Rudragaira Gad (stream), comes from the base of the Rudragaira peaks and meets the Bhagirathi at Bhaironghati.

The trail to Kedar Tal begins at Dandi chetra Gangotri and follows the course of the Kedar Ganga, keeping to its right bank. A trek of 7.5 km takes one to Bhoj Kharak. The steep climb is through a balmy pine forest. Just below Bhoj Kharak, clumps of Himalayan birch (bhoj) replace the pines, and there is a meadow suitable for camping.

The flesh-coloured bark of the bhoj was used by sages as paper—Bhoj patra—for their manuscripts before paper as such came into being. Many old manuscripts have been re-recorded from bhoj patra.

Another 4 km, above the tree line, is Kedar Kharak, another flat meadow where one can camp. This lap of the trek is sometimes hazardous because of recurrent rockfalls. Firewood is not available here.

Kedar Tal is still five kilometers away. The ascent is laborious through loose tumbled rocks. The best route keeps the Thalesagar peak in line of sight. The climb is steep and ridge after ridge appears. It seems an endless climb. The peaks of the Bhrigu Parvat and Rudragaira loom larger with the ascent.

Kedar Tal and its environs are sheer unspoilt nature—the charm soothes the weary traveller.

A ridge separates Kedar Tal from the Rudragaira Kharak. Rather than return the same way, one can cross the ridge to the other side, and return along the Rudragaira Gad. Negotiating the ridge takes five hours and is a trek of 5 km. The ridge, 700 meters higher than Kedar Tal, is a vantage point where a vast panorama of snowlands and lush green valleys unfolds itself to the eye.

Rudragaira Kharak is the base camp for the group of peaks above. The path keeps to the left of the Rudragaira Gad most of the way. When coming down the ridge the Rudragaira Gad should be crossed at the first available glacial bridge. The path is on the left bank while the right bank becomes a sheer cliff. Near Gangotri it is necessary to cross back, this time via a bridge. This should be done as early as possible because by the evening the bridge can be flooded by the melt from the glaciers. From here Gangotri is only approximately 2 km. It is possible to camp on the left bank if the bridge is flooded.

Bandar Punch viewed from the ridge above Khukala Tal.

The Local Lore of Sahastra Tal

THE uncommon pilgrimage to Sahastra Tal is an annual event for the villagers on both sides of the watershed dividing Uttarkashi and Tehri, interior districts of Garhwal. On either side there are seven sacred lakes, with the highest considered the holiest. Pilgrims visit the highest lakes on both sides, performing *puja* by the lakeside of their respective side then crossing the ridge to visit the other. From the Uttarkashi side, the villagers follow the Pilangana stream branching off at Shilla for the meadows of Kush Kalyan. Returning, there is a shorter way directly down the Pilangana valley past the isolated village of Johra. From the Tehri side, the villagers follow the Bhilangna and turn west at Gangi for the steep climb.

The word Sahastra, meaning "a thousand" in Sanskrit, was given to the area by wandering holy men, among the toughest of pilgrims. By their austere lifestyle most of them are fully acclimatised to the rigours of high altitude trekking. It is also the modification of the local Garhwali word *sahasyu* which means seven. The topmost and the largest lake on the Pilangana side is referred to as Darshan Tal. This aloof expanse of sapphire or emerald changes according to the glances of the sun. It is said by the villagers to contain the golden palace of Vishnu in the centre. During a full moon in the rainy season the villagers carry their god in a palanquin and worship him here on the auspicious occasion. No matter how freezing the weather the villagers will bathe in the lake.

The base for the seven lakes is called Dharamshala which refers to a primitive stone hut built for pilgrims, but unfortunately damaged by them. The roof timber has been pulled down and burnt at this exposed and windy site. The hut had been built by a district magistrate, who after undertaking the pilgrimage to Sahastra Tal was moved by the plight of the shivering pilgrims. The names of the other lakes in the series of the seven accomodates worshippers of Shiva as well as Vishnu, and Pari Tal "the lake of the fairies" caters to the local belief in nature spirits. The use of the name Darshan Tal for the highest lake satisfies Hindu orthodoxy while the other widely used name of Sahastra Tal, though very Sanskritic, also refers to unorthodox Tantra school which has always fascinated the village mind. The "thousand-petal lotus" of the mind is the goal of the mystical serpent power, the *kundalini* energy, as she flows up the spine of the yogi from his base nature to illuminate his understanding.

It would be surprising if the five Pandava brothers, the heroes of the Hindu epic, *The Mahabharata,* did not appear in this lake area or have natural features named after them. Between Dharamshala and Darshan Tal are the curious natural terraced "fields" of *Pandavasera* which are said to have been the rice paddies of the heroes of the old.

On the descent to the Bhilangna across the watershed, there are many more lakes and these include another sacred seven near the fascinating village of Gangi. Here we find the missing names : Arjuna Tal, Bhim Tal, referring to the Pandava brothers and Draupadi Tal to their shared wife.

The highest lake on the Bhilangna side called Gaumukhi Tal (or Vishnu Tal) is also the holiest. The trekker and/or pilgrim should tread carefully lest he anger the gods. A tale is told of a group of travellers in the region who did not bear this in mind. Ignoring the ban on alcohol, meat, etc., they were surprised by Vishnu in serpent form who unleashed a thunder storm with heavy rain and snow. All but one perished. He was spared to carry back the warning.

As in many locations in Garhwal, a small rivalry continues between Vishnu and Shiva, here Khatling on the Bhilangna side is the home of Shiva with many natural ice lingams appearing (according to locals) and Sahastra Tal is the home of Vishnu. It is interesting to note that Vishnu, the preserver, is associated with water in its liquid life-giving

Upper left—A palanquin carrying the local deity for puja at Darshan Tal. The two flowers are both commonly referred to as Himalayan Lotus. During the full moon of Bhadon (Aug/Sept) the villagers make this pilgrimage.

Middle left—Brahmkamal along the shores of Gaumukhi Tal.
Lower left—Darshan Tal viewed from the ridge dividing it and Gaumukhi Tal.

Page 65—Pilgrims from nearby villages performing Pitra Visarjana, a ceremony for the dead ensuring their passage to heaven.

Pages 66-67—The upper three lakes on the Bhilangna side. The largest is called Gaumukhi Tal.

form, and Shiva, the destroyer, with snow and ice, the destructive aspect of water.

Sahastra Tal Region Trek

Options:

1. Mala-Sahastra Tal-Gangi; gradual ascent-steep descent.
2. Gangi-Sahastra Tal-Mala; steep ascent-gradual descent.
3. Darshan Tal to Belak.
4. Return along same route; visiting the upper lakes of each group.
5. From Gangi continue onto Khatling.
6. From Gangi descend to Ghuttu return along Kedarnath-Gangotri yatra route or to Soneprayag.

From Ghuttu to Mala is the suggested route. From Ghuttu to Reeh is a 10 km gradual climb. Reeh to Gangi is a further 10 km gradual climb. Within 4 km beyond, and after descending to the Bhilangna and ascending to a hut and large rock, is a campsite. Beyond this is a bifurcation. The path along the river leads to Khatling Glacier. The path to the left leads up a steep hill through dense forests, this path leads to Sahastra Tal. From here it is 16 km to a rock shelter dharamshala ascending throughout. At times the path fades out and disappears. When this happens re-trace your steps and see where the path would logically go.

Note

This 16 km stretch should be done in one day and water should be carried.

From the rock shelter is a view of Gangi and Khatling Glacier. The rock shelter is also visible from Gangi. Above the rock shelter on the ridge to the right is a stream and campsite. To continue to Sahastra Tal, either return to the rock shelter, then climb the ridge directly above or walk along the ridge until above the rock shelter. From this location continue ascending the ridge and for the most part staying to the right. Gaumukhi Tal and two other lakes are a steep 6 km away. From Gaumukhi Tal to the top of the ridge is 1 km; then 1 km to Darshan Tal, the highest lake on the other side. These 2 km are both a steep ascent and a steep descent. Gradually descending 4 km is Dhudi Tal, a further 1 km steep descent is Pari Tal. From Pari Tal, along a rocky trail to the top of a ridge where there are stones piled up, (the ridge is called Khakhula Dhar), down to Khukhula Tal is 3 km. Over a small ridge of 1/2 km is Lum Tal and another 1 km gradual descent is Dharmashala.

Note

All these lakes are good campsites but of the upper two lakes Gaumukhi Tal (with a dharamshala) is a better location than Darshan Tal.

Dharamshala to Kharki (a good meadow camp) is 6 km gradual descent. While descending and following ridges keep to the left when a choice is necessary. Karki to Salmoth is 3 km. From here are two paths, one a steep descent 15 km via Kidhar, Jhoras and Shilla, and the other is via Chamin Chor, Papar then Shilla, gradual descent of 11 km. Shilla to Mala is 4 km.

Khatling Glacier

Situated between Gangotri and Kedarnath, not quite linking them, but along the route, is Khatling Glacier. It is the source of the Bhilangna and home of a cave where an ice lingam, similar to the one at Amarnath resides. According to the locals, many lingams exist, on the glacier.

Many villagers in the area know of the route from Gangotri to Kedarnath but none has followed it. When referring to Rudragaira, (the access point to Gangotri), most refer to the peak that is visible. Many have travelled the other way to Kedarnath via Maser Tal, Pain Tal and Vasuki Tal. Several expeditions have now crossed from Gangotri to Kedarnath. The pioneer of the trail was J.B. Auden who crossed in 1939. The connecting col is named after him.

The trek to Khatling begins at the roadhead at Ghuttu on the Bhilangna. This village is typical of any on a road that is not much used. It is a blend of a quiet village and a roadside village. After Ghuttu is Reeh, a village in contact with the modern world because of its proximity to Ghuttu and yet somewhat isolated. Then comes the truly isolated world of Gangi.

The small isolated village of Gangi lies along the route to Khatling Glacier. To many it represents one of the few remaining links with the past. Those who have visited it call it a living museum. It is like other villages in the upper reaches of Garhwal where accessibility is limited to those who live there or those who are out trekking or to the now rare breed of pilgrims crossing overland rather than by road. Gangi residents have seen very few visitors and very little of the modern world.

The village is divided into three regions. The lowest is where the winter homes are, the middle is the main village where the villagers live most of the time. And the highest part is for the summer when the upper grasses and cool air provide the best grazing grounds for the animals.

Because of the isolation the villagers have had to have inter-marriage. This has also kept the population down but this was not one of their objectives. Villages around Gangi are jealous of the relative prosperity of those living in Gangi and have tended to make up stories, some of them quite exaggerated.

The holy river Bhilangna, according to legend, is actually a maiden who tried to capture Shiva's attention while he meditated and upon being rebuked was dissolved into water. According to the locals, there are seven Shivlingas at Bondobali Tal. And in the age-old tradition of the Rishis and sages fleeing the world for the upper reaches of the Himalaya there is an Ashram where Bhrigu Rishi stays.

To the north, crossing over to Rudragaira involves more strenuous effort. After Gangi is Kharsoli, a Gujjar settlement. The valley leading to Kharsoli is covered with a profusion of flowers seen at their best during the monsoons. After passing a waterfall one comes to a rock projection known as Khatling cave. The last pasture land of the Gujjars is called Kachotra and is almost the last of

the green. Along this way it is possible to walk along the divide of the glacier but after Kachotra more and more of snow and ice must be crossed.

It is not until after the second bend and until climbing to 5,000 m that the col is visible. The view of this area is of several glaciers as well as the major peaks in the Gangotri region. Prominent peaks are Jaonli and Gangotri.

Going south from Khatling after 6 km one reaches Maser Tal, a lake 4 km in circumference. After 2 km are ridges and after 1 km after this is Pain Tal. Three kilometres, downhill, brings the trekker to Vasuki Tal and downhill 6 km more is Kedarnath. Vasuki Tal is half the size of Maser Tal.

Kedarnath—Gangotri Yatra Route

Kedarnath lies 17 km, from Gaurikund along

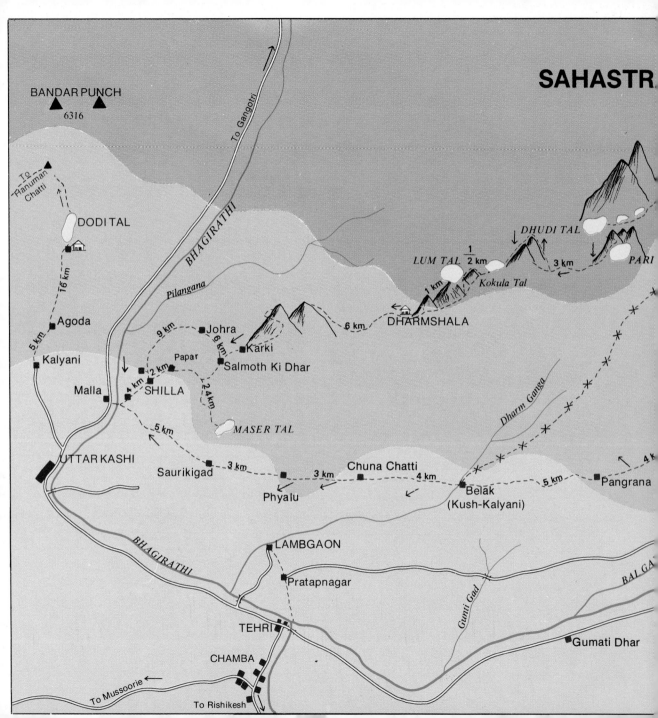

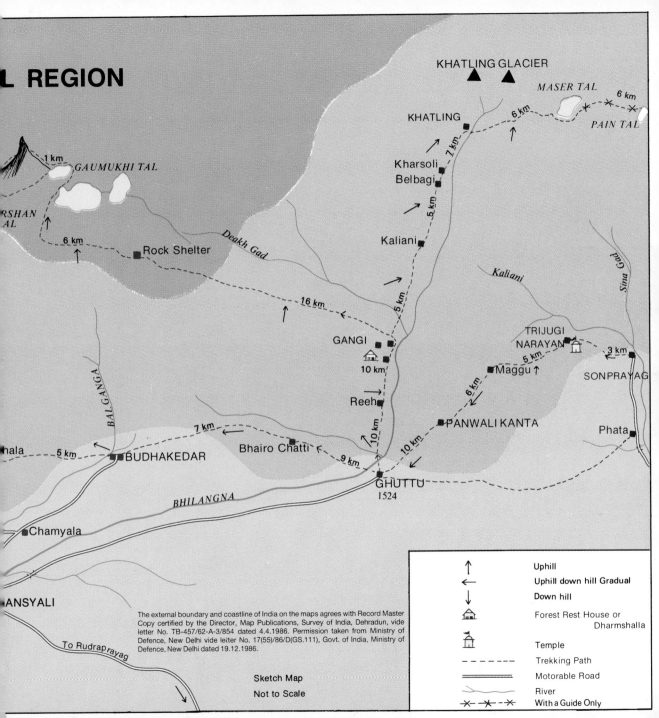

L REGION

KHATLING GLACIER

MASER TAL

6 km

KHATLING

6 km

PAIN TAL

1 km

GAUMUKHI TAL

Kharsoli
Belbagi

7 km

5 km

Deakh Gad

6 km

Rock Shelter

RSHAN AL

Kaliani

Kaliani

Sina Gad

16 km

5 km

TRIJUGI
NARAYAN

3 km

GANGI

10 km

SONPRAYAG

Reeh

Maggu

5 km

6 km

BAL GANGA

7 km

10 km

PANWALI KANTA

Phata

hala

5 km

Bhairo Chatti

9 km

10 km

BUDHAKEDAR

GHUTTU
1524

BHILANGNA

Chamyala

ANSYALI

To Rudraprayag

The external boundary and coastline of India on the maps agrees with Record Master
Copy certified by the Director, Map Publications, Survey of India, Dehradun, vide
letter No. TB-457/62-A-3/854 dated 4.4.1986. Permission taken from Ministry of
Defence, New Delhi vide letter No. 17(55)/86/D(GS.111), Govt. of India, Ministry of
Defence, New Delhi dated 19.12.1986.

Sketch Map

Not to Scale

↑	Uphill
←	Uphill down hill Gradual
↓	Down hill
🏠	Forest Rest House or Dharmshalla
🚩	Temple
- - - - -	Trekking Path
═══	Motorable Road
	River
–x–x–x–	With a Guide Only

a gradually ascending path. It is possible to trek 11 km to Rambara (Tourist Bungalow and chatties) then continue in the morning. These next 3 km are the steepest. The other 3 km is a gradual ascent.

The old yatra route is exhausting but offers glimpses of village life off the motor roads. It begins at Mala along the motor road, 73 km below Gangotri. Sauri-ki-gad is a very gradual descent of 5 km. A steep 3 km ascent leads to Phaylu. Another 3 km descent is Chunachatti followed by a steep ascent 4 km to Belak. From Belak a 5 km gradual descent is Pangrana, followed by a gradual 4 km ascent to Jhala. Budh Kedar is a further 5 km descent. A slight descent for 4 km is Tolachatti. Then a steep 3 km ascent leads to Bhaironchatti. A 9 km descent is Ghuttu (this is the roadhead from Tehri). A very steep 9 km ascent finds Panwali. After a 6 km gradual descent is Maggu (this path covers difficult rocky terrain). Triyoginarayan is another 5 km descent. The first part is steep the rest is gradual. Three km

Two lakes along the high altitude route connecting Khatling Glacier and Kedarnath Temple. As with many lakes local pilgrims travel here to do puja.

further is Soneprayag. From here it is possible to take a bus, jeep or taxi to Gaurikund or to continue trekking. Gaurikund-Kedarnath is described above.

Note:

Chattis and Dharamshalas exist in all these villages. Some may not be in the best condition but a tent or extra rations need not to be taken unless desired.

Options:

1. From Belak crossing up to the Sahastra Tal region.
2. From Ghuttu climbing to Khatling Glacier and returning to Gangotri via Audens Col and Rudragaira or continuing to Kedarnath via Maser Tal, Pain Tal and Vasuki Tal.
3. From Ghuttu to Phata.

High Altitude Route via Khatling Glacier.

Best done June-Sept(earlier or later depending on snowfall). From Gangotri follow the Rudragaira gad 20 km to the base camp for Rudragaira peaks. Ascend to Audens col then descend along Khatling Glacier. From Khatling it is 6 km to Masar Tal, then 1 km to a ridge followed by 7 km to Painya Tal. Vasuki Tal lies 2 more km below; another 6 km descent leads to Kedarnath.

Kedarkhand: Abode Of Shiva

The Panch Kedars

THE uppermost reaches of the Garhwal Himalaya are called Kedarkhand, the abode of Shiva. The large number of temples dedicated to Shiva, dotted all over, are ample testimony of the extent of influence of the Shiva cult.

Lord Shiva, a member of the Holy Trinity of the Hindu faith, is the "destroyer". He is known by many more names and attitudes. But he is more popularly associated with his symbol, the lingam (phallus). Fertility cults were very predominant in this region and by incorporation of the worship of the lingam, and its female counterpart, the yoni, Hinduism was able to increase its following.

Many believe that the temples of Kedar had little to do with each other until later. While Shankaracharaya was trekking through the area, he discovered these temples, with their cults of worshippers. After recounting the story of Shiva's flight from the Pandavas, he identified these particular locations as the places where the parts of Shiva re-emerged. Shankaracharaya thereby put concrete form to the legend by identifying the temples and gathered and incorporated the various fertility cults together under Hinduism.

The Kedarnath Temple is the largest building before the glacier. When built the glacier was directly behind the temple. It is receding as are all glaciers in this area, leaving a trail of rocky debris in their wake.

73

With winter the Kedarnath temple closes and a representative image is carried down to the Okimath temple. These two temples, both homes to Shiva, are similar, differing only in elevation. The austere stone temple at Okimath contrasts with its brightly painted gate.

Facing page—Although tridents are commonly found throughout Garhwal, this one is unique because it is in the Nepalese art style. It is believed that this trident was placed by the Gurkhas sometime during their conquests.

The legend of the Panch Kedars begins with the battle of Kurukshetra, recounted in the Mahabharata, between the Kauravas and the Pandavas. The Pandavas, after killing the Kauravas, realised their sin and sought absolution. After a trip to Kashi they were refused forgiveness by Mahadev (as Shiva is called there). Shiva left the area and led the Pandavas on an extensive chase through most of the Garhwal Himalaya. It was at Kedarnath that Shiva was finally traced. Working on the assumption that Shiva may have turned himself into a buffalo and was in the midst of the herd, Bhim waited until sunset when the herd would return home, then he straddled the valley as the buffaloes passed underneath. The astute Bhim knew that if Shiva had taken the form of a buffalo he would not allow anyone to mount his back (even in this fashion). The buffalo that refused to pass was Shiva. Bhim grabbed Shiva just as he dove under the ground and because he was strong Bhim was able to hold on to part of Shiva. The hindquarters remained and are still worshipped at Kedarnath. The other parts re-emerged at the other temples, the belly or navel at Madmaheshwar, the arms at Tungnath, the face at Rudranath, and the matted locks at Kalpeshwar.

A pilgrim to the Panch Kedars should follow the sequence of their establishment, Kedarnath, Madmaheshwar, Tungnath, Rudranath and Kalpeshwar. This particular pilgrimage is recommended for absolution from the sin of slaughtering a cow. However, any variety of routes can be followed using bus or foot, at the traveller's discretion.

The Rawal (head priest) at the main Kedarnath temple is considered to be the living embodiment of God. At Madmaheshwar the priest is called the Maha Guru. The pandas for all but Kalpeshwar come from villages around Guptakashi, Okhimath, and Mokumath. Since all but the Kalpeshwar temple are located at high altitudes, the temple doors are ceremoniously closed in the autumn to be re-opened with the spring. Symbolic images are carried down at the closing from Kedarnath and Madmaheshwar to Okhimath, from Tungnath to Mokumath, and from Rudranath to Gopeshwar.

Around the main Kedar shrine are a number of sites of religious significance. The *samadhi* of Shankaracharaya is located at the back of the temple. Approximately 3/4 km away is Chorabari Tal now referred to as Gandhi Sarovar. The Mahatma's ashes were submerged here. On the right of the temple is a cliff know as Mahapanth (pathway to Heaven). The mountain itself is called Bhrigu Panth, while the cliff is also called Bhairava Jhamp. Similar to the English 'jump', this is where ritual suicide by *yatris* took place. Many felt that this was a means of attaining *moksha*. The would-be suicide inscribed his name at Gopeshwar. According to British accounts, as many as 15,000 yatris leapt to their death each year. Obviously this is an exaggeration, but certainly several could have done so.

Of interest around the other temples, (needless to say), is the view. Tungnath is the highest temple in Garhwal and all of

India at 3,680 metres. Behind the temple, an hour's walk away, is the peak of Chandershilla, 3,930 m, which offers a panorama both to the east and the west.

Panch Kedar Trek

Many possible directions for trekking are open. Also various combinations using bus.

Options:

1. By bus, minimum of trekking. Guptakashi-Madmaheshwar-30 km. Return by

Sunrise near the Madmaheshwar Temple reflected on the snows of the Chaukhaba peaks.

Right—Another sunrise, another peak. Nanda Devi, one of the most elusive and seductive of peaks, is silhouetted here. She is a difficult peak to view because the sentinel peaks compose a curtain, sheltering her from view. This glimpse is from the buggyals before Rudranath.

Following page—As the storm clouds gather, the snows continue to revel in their own glory. Weather is always unpredictable at high altitudes. Pictured are Yamunotri-Gangotri peaks at left, Chaukhamba peaks at right.

same route or follow trail at Lank to Deoria Tal 4 1/2 km more than to Guptakashi. Mastura or Guptakashi to Chopta by bus Chopta-Tungnath 3 km. Chopta to Mandal or Gopeshwar by bus Rudranath 20 km. Mandal or Gopeshwar to Helang by bus Helang to Kalpeshwar 10 1/2 km.

2. Bus part trek part; by Bus—Gopeshwar or Mandal to Chopta. Chopta to Guptakashi or Mastura, by foot-Helang-Kal-

peshwar–Dumak–Rudranath–Mandal–(Gopeshwar). Chopta–Tungnath Mastura–Deoria-Tal–Madmaheshwar or Guptakashi–Madmaheshwar.

3. Trek all of it (Guptakashi to Gaurikund by bus).

Route described from Helang: All by trek. From Helang descend to and cross the Alaknanda. Gradual ascent for 9 km along mule-track (several obvious shortcuts cover terrain unsuitable for animals) to Urgam. Kalpeshwar is 1-1/2 km further up the valley and across the river. Returning to just above Urgam, the path bifurcates to the right ascends the pass, 3400 m and slightly descends to Dumak, 17 km total. (2-3 km before Dumak are a meadow campsite or a dharamshala by a temple across the river).

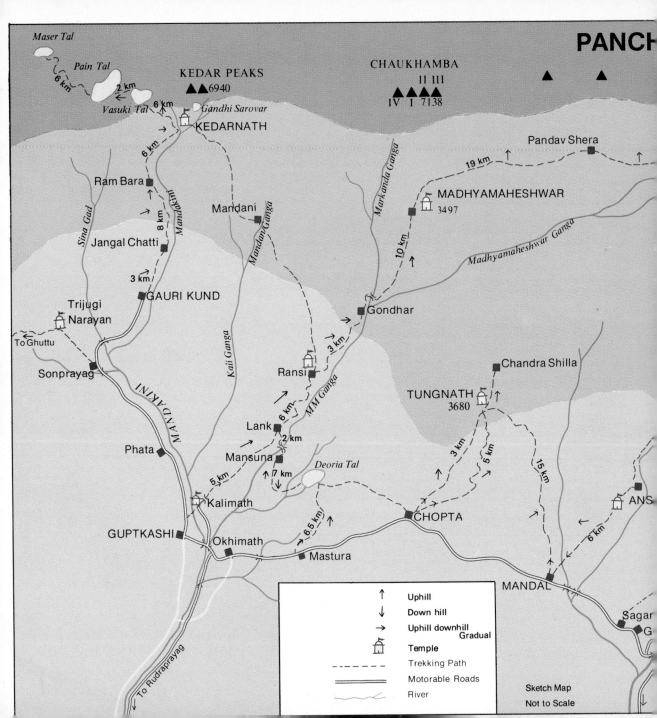

Maser Tal

Pain Tal

6 km

2 km

Vasuki Tal

6 km

KEDAR PEAKS

▲▲6940

Gandhi Sarovar

KEDARNATH

CHAUKHAMBA

II III

▲▲▲▲

IV I 7138

PANCH

Pandav Shera

6 km

Ram Bara

Mandani

19 km

MADHYAMAHESHWAR

3497

Markanda Ganga

Sina Gad

8 km

Mandakini

Mandani Ganga

10 km

Madhyamaheshwar Ganga

Jangal Chatti

3 km

GAURI KUND

Trijugi
Narayan

To Ghuttu

Sonprayag

MANDAKINI

Kali Ganga

Gondhar

3 km

Ransi

MM Ganga

Chandra Shilla

TUNGNATH
3680

3 km

5 km

15 km

Phata

5 km

Lank

2 km

Mansuna

7 km

Deoria Tal

ANS

6 km

Kalimath

CHOPTA

6.5 km

GUPTKASHI

Okhimath

Mastura

MANDAL

Sagar

G

To Rudraprayag

	Uphill
↓	Down hill
→	Uphill downhill Gradual
🛕	Temple
- - -	Trekking Path
═══	Motorable Roads
∼∼∼	River

Sketch Map
Not to Scale

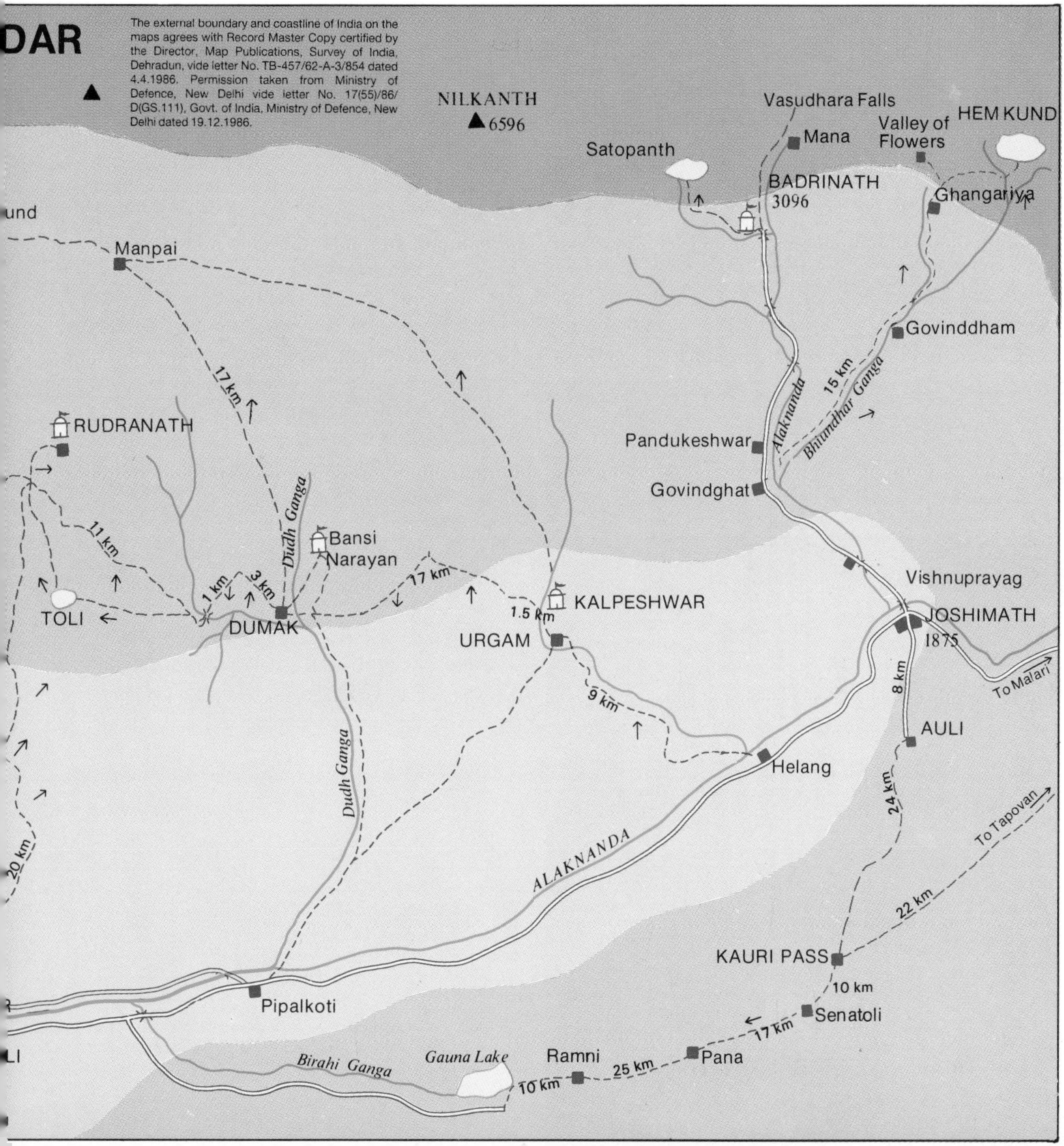

DAR
The external boundary and coastline of India on the maps agrees with Record Master Copy certified by the Director, Map Publications, Survey of India, Dehradun, vide letter No. TB-457/62-A-3/854 dated 4.4.1986. Permission taken from Ministry of Defence, New Delhi vide letter No. 17(55)/86/ D(GS.111), Govt. of India, Ministry of Defence, New Delhi dated 19.12.1986.
NILKANTH
6596
Vasudhara Falls
Mana
Valley of Flowers
HEM KUND
Satopanth
BADRINATH
3096
Ghangariya
und
Manpai
Govinddham
17 km
15 km
Alaknanda
Bhiundhar Ganga
RUDRANATH
Pandukeshwar
Govindghat
11 km
Dudh Ganga
Bansi Narayan
17 km
1 km
3 km
Vishnuprayag
TOLI
DUMAK
1.5 km
KALPESHWAR
JOSHIMATH
1875
URGAM
8 km
To Malari
9 km
AULI
Helang
24 km
Dudh Ganga
To Tapovan
20 km
ALAKNANDA
22 km
KAURI PASS
10 km
Pipalkoti
Senatoli
17 km
LI
Birahi Ganga
Gauna Lake
Ramni
Pana
25 km
10 km

From Dumak 3 km along the ridge, 1 km descending to the Duddh Ganga. The path ends and one should continue upstream along the river. There are two bridges; one is made of 4 or 5 logs, the other is a wide log. The wide log is beyond the big rock with a log ladder climbing it. The smaller 4-5 log bridge may be washed away depending on the time of year.

After crossing, head straight up through very dense jungle and after 25-30 m the main path should be located. This ascends through gradually thinning underbrush and jungle until the tree-line is reached. Once on top in the buggyal, Rudranath is 3 km to the right.

Note—from Dumak this should be done in one day until the tree-line and buggyal.

Returning 3 km from Rudranath, is the crossroads where the Dumak, Gopeshwar and Mandal trails meet. For Gopeshwar, continue straight and ascend the ridge and continue for 17 km. For Mandal bifurcate on the left and zig-zag up the ridge. Continue a very steep descent 8 km to Naila (Gujjar settlement). Slightly less steep descent 6 km

Upper left—The temple complex at Rudranath. The sanctum sanctorum is on the far right. The outer smaller buildings house other deities and local devta idols.

Bottom left—Tungnath Temple, the highest temple in India, lies at an elevation of 3680 m. From Chandershilla peak, behind the temple, a 180° view of the Himalaya covering all the major peaks in Garhwal.

Facing page—Harvest time near the temple village of Ransi. Although flowers are usually considered the most colourful plants in the Garhwal, the simple beauty of ripening grain fields should not be overlooked.

to a dudh-wala's (milk man), home then down to cross the river and continue to Ansuya Devi 3 km. Mandal is a further 6 km gradual descent.

Above Mandal, 1 km along the foot-path (cuts across the road) is a F.R.H. Pangar Basa. Another 14 km is Chopta and 5 or 3 km (depending on the path) is Tungnath.

Returning to Chopta descend 9 km to Dogal-bitta. A further 16 km descent is Deoria Tal. First descending then ascending 7 km is Mansuna. After crossing the Madmaheshwar Ganga is Lank, 4 km. After 6 km is Ransi and a further 3 km is Gaundhar. The last ascent of 10 km (carry water) is Madmaheshwar. Nineteen kilometers from Madmaheshwar is Nandi Kund and two routes returning to Urgam or to Dumak.

Returning along the same route, from Madmaheshwar at Lank, follow the trail to the right for 5 km to reach Kalimath. Six more km is Guptakashi.

Dev Bhumi:
Vishnu's Valley

The Panch Badris

BADRINATH, the shrine of Lord Vishnu, is considered one of the holiest in India. Until recently it was also the most inaccessible. Now with a motor road to the temple door, the weary and the dangerous trails for the footsore villagers can be avoided but at the price that the other four temples dedicated to Badrinath tend to be bypassed. The word *Badri* is derived from a wild fruit which Vishnu was said to have lived on when he did penance in Badrivan, the area which covers all five temples. Shankaracharya, the monist philosopher, is credited with establishing the four great pilgrimages of India in the early ninth century AD. Possibly Badrinath was chosen for its hot springs, for this refreshing climax to a long trek worked wonders on the hardy old breed of pilgrims. The looming background beauty of the Neel-kanth peak adds to the majesty of the Mana valley and the surrounding holy places, named after the heroes of Hindu mythology, who become convincingly alive if approached with a pilgrim's faith. The main Badrinath shrine is small, and darshan of the Lord Badri Vishal is always a crowded affair. The Rawal (head priest) hails from the Namboodri village in Kerala, the birthplace of Shanka-racharya. The tiny bazaar is a fascinating reminder of the old hill culture. In winter all the villagers move down the valley. Although Badrinathji is worshipped at Pandu-keshwar, the actual image is left, for during the winter the Gods worship it.

Unlike the Panch Kedar temples which are at high altitudes, the Panch Badris are situated in the valleys, and opinions vary on their actual sites. The main shrine of Badri Vishal, Yogdhyan Badri at Panduke-shwar and the curious Bhavishya Badri are undisputed. Adi Badri seems too far from the other temple to constitute part of a circuit, and some authorities hold that a temple at Urgam is the claimant to the title. Also, the claims of Vriddha Badri, the old temple of Animath, are said to be over-shadowed by the presence of Nar Singh temple in Joshimath, where the Rawal spends his winters. If one were a pilgrim, it would be logical in Urgam to pass from the last of the five Kedars to the first of the five Badri temples, and then proceed along the north bank of the Alaknanda to Panduke-shwar and Badrinath. Returning over the river at Vishnuprayag, the pilgrim could continue the circuit via the hot springs below

Sevai (Tapovan) then reach Joshimath.

Architecturally, the most interesting Badri temple is the cluster at Adi Badri near Karanprayag. The most ancient appears to be at Pandukeshwar downstream from the main temple. Here is Yogdhyan Badri, Vishnu in meditation. The fourth Badri at Animath is called Vriddha Badri which means the ancient form of the deity. It was here that Shankaracharya is believed to have first re-enshrined the idol of Badrinathji. By far the most mysterious because of its inaccessibility is Bhavishya Badri, the temple of the future Lord Badrinath. To find this tiny temple one has to climb from Tapovan (another site of hot springs) for fourteen kilometers until a dense forest of spruce is reached under the snow peaks of Nanda Devi Sanctuary. Hidden in this forest is a small spring which is said to be increasing in its flow just as the image of Nar Singh in the Joshimath temple is said to have an arm which is growing thinner. When that arm breaks, the two mountains guarding the approach to Badrinath will collapse to block

Preceding page—Closing prayers at the Badrinath Temple. The Rawal (head priest) ceremoniously closes the temple doors each winter and vacates the area allowing the devtas and gods to come and worship here.

A bird's-eye view of the Alaknanda passing through the village of Badrinath. The temple (far right center) is a gaudy splash of colour in predominantly grey surroundings.

the road. Then the Bhavishya Badri temple will become the main shrine. These legends were perhaps prompted by the narrow frightening ledges along which the old pilgrim trails passed. One interesting modern observation is that the beautiful spruce jungle above Tapovan must have been how the site resembled Badrivan—the forest of Badrinath—as Shankaracharya knew it. Over the centuries the trees have all been felled for fuel. Without the hot springs the pilgrimage would have been an even more hazardous undertaking.

Nowadays most pilgrims consider the main shrine their goal and the other four temples are sadly neglected. Adi Badri lies on the motor road between Karanprayag and Ranikhet but most pilgrims take the Rishikesh road. The bus passes close to Vriddha Badri and Yogdhyan Badri. Most modern pilgrims prefer to avoid the extra walking entailed. Even the sites around the main temple are now less visited. On the hill above the temple in full view of the majesty of Neelkanth is the rock Charanpaduka with Vishnu's footprint impressed on it. Around the village of Mana, the last village in India, is the cave where Vyasa is said to have written commentaries on the great epic poems of Hinduism.

With all these vibrant mythological associations, the pilgrimage was a total experience and for many the goal of a life time. The full beauty of the meditating Vishnu and the greatness of Badri Vishal was only revealed to those who had made strenuous

Facing page—Nilkanth, the guardian of the Badrinath Temple is silent witness to the darshan of the gods and devtas during winter.

A representative idol is carried to Pandukeshwar, one of the Panch Badri temples called Yogdhyan (meditating) Badri. The Badris are temples dedicated to Vishnu and the legend about their original consecration of the Badrinath Temple includes an agreement that for half the year Vishnu be worshipped in his sringaric (decorative) form by mortals, and in his yogdhyani (meditative) form by the gods.

efforts to reach his feet. The circuit of the five temples was a ritual of discipline to guarantee that the pilgrim would not forget the many faces and moods of the inscrutable Godhead, for the experience taught him that the temples along the way are many, but the goal is one.

The Valley of Flowers is described in local myth as the home of fairies that will spirit away the unknowing shepherd who enters. The early morning mist over the peaks give credence to this myth.

Facing page—Brahamkamal (Saussurea obvallata)—the yellow Himalayan Lotus surrounded by lesser flowers as if in worship as the base of the only flower which is a fit offering to the gods.

Of Hindu Myth and Sikh Legend

The Valley of Flowers

THE Valley of Flowers has been described as "Nature's Rock Garden". This is both misleading and incorrect. Incorrect because the label limits the magnitude and scope of the valley and misleading to visitors. Many arrive at the valley expecting a cultivated garden which though wild in its nature is still controlled as a true rock garden

Above—Two horses coming for a drink near the falls seemingly unaware of their surroundings. The yellow flowers are Inula Grandiflora.

Middle left—The blue Himalayan Poppy (Meconopsis/latifolia).

Middle right—Cyananthus lobatus.

Far right—Potentilla/Astrosagvinea.

would be. This is not the case. Adjectives are pointless and redundant when describing Garhwal and nowhere is this more apparent then when describing the many valleys and buggyals decorated with multitudes of flowers. So instead of extolling the beauty and stupendous array of wild flowers growing here, a simple description and history will follow.

Credit for discovery of the valley goes

to Frank Smythe, the leader of a successful expedition, who took this route after climbing Mt. Kamet, in 1931. He later returned and collected many species of flowers which were carried back to England. His observation were recorded in a book simply titled *The Valley of Flowers* (which has been recently reprinted). Inspired by his writings and continuing his work, Joan Margaret Legge, lived in the valley for many months and fell to her death here (July 4, 1939). Her tombstone is placed near the center of the valley with the inscription:

"I will lift up mine eyes unto the hills from whence cometh my help"

Locally the valley has been known for centuries with its own myths surrounding it. Many will not enter for fear of fairies

carrying them away. It may well be that shepherds have entered the valley, and due to the high concentration of carbon dioxide or even the scent of certain flowers, have fallen asleep never to awaken. The valley is locally known as the Bhunder valley. The Pashupawati flows through the valley.

The diversity of flowers in such a small area is truly phenomenal. Research is still needed to fully understand the interrelationships between the plants, flowers and trees in the area. To name all of the flowers in the valley would require pages. A rough estimate of the known flowers numbers in the hundreds. Many other species have yet to be discovered or have been totally destroyed by the careless tread of visitors. These are but a few of the names: Anemones, Asters, Androsa, Borage, Cypripedium, Forget-me-nots, Blue poppies, Fritillaria,

Upper left—These flowers abound throughout the valley.
Middle left—Edelweiss, a popular European alpine flower.
Lower left—This flower is also commonly referred to as Himalayan Lotus and is ritually offered during puja—Savssurea Gramini Folia.

Page 97—The Pashupawati flows through the center of the Valley and meets with the Lakshman Ganga near Ghangariya.

Geraniums, Dwarf Iris, Dwarf Larkspur, Rhododendrons, Primulas (which Smythe raved about) and Brahamkamal.

Two Hindu myths are centred around the Valley. During the period of the Rama-yana, Hanuman the monkey god, was des-patched by Lord Rama to get the herb, Sanjivini butti, which would save the life of his younger brother, Lakshman. Hanuman, unable to identify the herb, uprooted an entire mountain in this area and brought it back to Lord Rama. The other myth centers around the always popular Pandavas. While travelling through this region Draupadi spot-ted a Brahamkamal floating down the Laksh-man Ganga. So taken was she by the beauty of the flower that she requested Bhim to go find where the flower had originated from. Bhim climbed up the valley through the dense forest and coming to a junction of two streams followed the one on the left, the Pashupawati, which has its source at the glacier at the back of the valley. He followed the stream and came to a valley filled with flowers and among them was the Brahamkamal (this flower is used by the Hindus in their puja) and in the first act of conservation associated with the valley plucked *one* Brahamkamal to bring back with his account of a floral valley surpassing the beauty of any other on earth.

An apt description by Dr. Thomas Longs-taff, a famous mountaineer, is found in his book, *This is My Voyage*. He looked down into a valley that was the richest green balm to the eyes after the stony desolation he had left behind. They reached it on July 13 to find the most luxuriant meadows within this part of the Himalaya. They waded through flowers upto their waist, ferns, yellow lilies and anemones, green fritillarias, purple monk's hood, blue dwarf irises, masses of forget-me-nots with yellow king cups by the stream. Innumerable butterflies of alpine forms, including at least two species of large swallow-tails, with many singing birds, were about them on all sides. They found a spot of grassy swad for tents, all unspoilt by sheep for, as the Garhwalis said, no flocks could be pastured there because of dungri bhik, and aconite which is poison to them. He found the charms of the place so irresis-table that he spent a whole day there.

Hemkund Sahib

Near the Valley of Flowers is Hemkund Sahib, at an atitude of 4, 150 m, sacred to both Sikhs and Hindus. The Sikhs revere this place because their tenth Guru described its location in his holy writings, the Dasam Sahib (the book of the Tenth Guru), as a location where he meditated. Some historians hold that the Tenth Guru, Guru Gobind Singh, actually visited this place and was able to describe it because he had retreated there. They contend that Guru Gobind Singh sought refuge from the Raja of Garhwal at Srinagar but was refused because the Raja feared the Mughals and wished peace to reign in his kingdom. The best he could offer the fleeing Guru was the anonymity of the Himalaya. The Guru accepted this little and retreated to higher regions and settled for a time near the shores of the lake surrounded by seven snow peaks. This location was not suitable for the Guru and he chose the possibility of prosecution to be near his people again. He used this time to prepare for his next attack against the Mughals raising an army at Paunta Sahib in the Dehra Dun Valley.

The writings of Guru Gobind Singh claim that he meditated there in a past life. If it seems strange that a Guru should claim to have had more than one life, Guru Gobind Singh has an explanation for that too. He was asked by God to come to the Earth again and be a Guru for his people and even though he did not want to he was prevailed upon to do so. Either of these reasons makes the spot of sacred significance to the Sikhs. The scenery alone is worthy of the pilgrimage.

For the Hindu the lake is known as Lokpal. Here, Lakshman, the younger brother of Lord Rama, meditated. A small temple is dedicated to Lakshman and it stands next to the new gurudwara under construction.

The lake was discovered in 1930 by Havildar Sohan Singh and since then it has become a major tourist attraction. The trail is lined with 'Chai' shops and no one goes for wanting thanks to the hospitality of the Gurudwara. Glasses of chai (tea) and *langer* (free food for all) are available as well as lodgings for the night.

The Sikhs have been the biggest influence on tourism in this area. It is mainly due to their effort that accommodation is available along this trek and the one to the Valley of the Flowers (they follow the same route till Ghangariya or Govind dham).

The lake has been the refuge for many seeking salvation through penance and meditation. King Pandu was said to have visited here to do penance. Even today the spellbinding qualities of the lake remain, in spite of the heavy flow of pilgrims.

Valley of Flowers and Hemkund Treks

The trek to Valley of Flowers is relatively easy, as it is to Hemkund except for the last 6 km. The route is the same for both until Ghangariya (Govind Dham). From Govind Ghat(the road-head) cross the Alaknanda and continue for a 15 km gradual climb.

To the Valley of Flowers it is a 4 km gradual ascent following the path to the left after Ghangariya. This is the entrance to the valley. The majority of the flowers are behind this weed barrier. The valley extends for 10 km. Through the center there is a path.

To Hemkund it is a 6 km steep ascent reaching 4150 m.

Note

Unless travelling with a tent and rations, trekkers must return to Ghangariya for the night. Ghangariya can be used as the base for day treks to both locations and a tent is not necessary.

Facing page—Hemkund Sahib—is the location described by the 10th Guru of the Sikhs, Guru Gobind Singh. Hemkund means snow lake and it was described as being surrounded by seven peaks.

Upper right—The steep accent to Hemkund Sahib is annually made by thousands of Sikhs of all ages. Entire villages travel together and trudge up behind the inspiring banner of the faith.

Middle right—Just as Ganga water is purifying for Hindus the icy cold water of the lake at Hemkund is purifying for Sikhs who immerse themselves in its water. Dips are taken for family members unable to make the pilgrimage.

Lower right—The small Hindu shrine dedicated to Lakshman, brother of Rama, who meditated here. The lake is traditionally called Lokpal.

The temple of Nanda Devi, is the last major Hindu temple before the Tibetan border. Lotus have been drawn flanking the entry and 'OM' the first syllable (sound) in the universe is painted above.

Facing page—One of the methods for transporting gear into the sanctuary is on the backs of goats who go there to graze. The route into the Sanctuary at places is little better than a goat track and in some places seems fit only for goats.

Nanda Devi: The Mountain Goddess

THE goddess Nanda means "she who gives bliss" and in both Kumaon and Garhwal, villagers worship her as Devi, the beautiful mother who removes their sufferings and bestows her blessings. The ancient fertility cult of Ufrey Devi may indicate the origins of the Nanda myth, for its centre lies at Ufrey Tak, a hill above the famous Nauti village, where the most famous of the Nanda Devi pilgrimages starts. The Nautiyals who organise the twelve-yearly *Bara Nanda Jat* to the base of the Nanda Devi Sanctuary curtain, are the gurus to the Garhwal Maharaja and their influence dates from the fourteenth century. They came with the royal court from the plains of western India to seek refuge in the hills from the savage attacks of Mohammed of Ghazni.

The pre-brahminical religion they founded was the fertility cult of the mother goddess, common to all rural societies, and the worship of nature spirits known as *devtas*. One of

the places the Nanda Devi pilgrimage passes is Wan, which possesses a huge and remarkable lone deodar tree in the midst of a cypress forest. This gnarled and timeless tree is the home of Latu Maharaj, a *devta*. It seems many of the gods and *devtas* began as canonised local heroes, and it is quite possible Nanda Devi also was remembered as a kind princess who perhaps died young. In the annual fair in her honour many worship her as a princess who was killed by a buffalo. During the celebrations it was traditional to slaughter this animal. Clearly the story ties in with the worship of the Hindu goddess Durga, who slaughters demons with her trident and is offered animal sacrifices at the Dusherra festival, the most famous example being the blood offerings of the Gurkhas who are, of course, hill neighbours of the Nanda Devi region.

Nowadays in towns the buffalo is spared but in the interior the bloodthirsty rites continue unabated. When the Nauti priests arrange their famous pilgrimage to the snows, other villages also send their goddesses in the procession. The core area of the Nanda Devi cult is around the foothills of the Nandakini, the river of the goddess which starts where the Nauti pilgrimage ends. Krur is a fascinating example where the goddess Nanda is regarded as a hill woman, who spends six months in her parents' home and the rest of the year with her in-laws. The fertility aspect of the seasonal change are obvious, for many villagers sow their wheat in winter and travel to lower elevations, returning to harvest the crop after six months when the sun has returned.

In a curious modern touch of drama to the undying legend of Nanda's beauty and benevolence, came the Unsoelds, father and daughter, from America, to climb the mountain in 1976. Actually the daughter had worked in the Himalaya, knew the language and was loved by the villagers. Her father was so taken by the beauty of the mountain that he called his daughter "Nanda Devi" Unsoeld. The expedition neared the top and then for no reason, while near the summit, the girl of twenty-four years suddenly died and became one with the mountain—as though the goddess had returned to her real home. Apparently, when the mountain was first climbed in 1936, the famous Tilman remarked on a snow pigeon that flew away as the summit was reached. In 1981, the mountain yielded to a woman. The lucky climber was Rekha Sharma from India who also was young and beautiful.

In all the villages the bards continue to sing the praises of Nanda Devi during her festivals and show interesting variations in the myth, seeing the goddess as two sisters in Kumaon where the twin peaks are·visible, and as one in Joshimath where the main peak alone can be viewed. In her temples the goddess is usually depicted with a silver mask, of a woman adorned with the heavy jewellery of the hill woman as she leaves her parent's home for her journey to the snows.

The goddess in her sanctuary remains aloof and unapproachable. The unique flora and fauna of this little visited paradise have earned for it the status of a biosphere preserved for posterity. This most beautiful of wilderness areas will remain to remind us of the full magic of the Himalaya.

Nanda Devi Trek

She is considered by many to be the most desirable mountain in the world. Her admirers range from tough explorers to simple villagers. Mountaineers cannot rest till they reach her twin summits (and few have reached both) while villagers mount pilgrimages to her outer curtain. Nanda Devi could not be approached until 1934 because of the ring of snow peaks around her sanctuary and the impenetrability of her only access, the Rishi Ganga gorge. The route carved out by Shipton and Tilman with their three invincible sherpas is still used by modern visitors. It starts with a killingly steep pull from the village of Lata at 1,500 m to Lata Kharak at 4,000 m. Leaving the magnificent conifer forests the trail now winds up and over the exposed Dharansi Pass at 4,667 m crossing the watershed of the Dhauli Ganga into the Rishi Ganga which marks the Outer Sanctuary. From the Malatuni Curtain with its prodigious view of Nanda Devi dwarfing the plummeting depths of the Rishi gorge, the trail drops sheer for 1,000 m to the lovely alp of Dibrugheta, amidst more spruce. A short climb brings one to a glorious view of the soaring loveliness of the mountain

goddess then down to the crossing point of the Rishi at Deodhi. The Rishi is a violent watchdog of the goddess, and to cross her demands a decisive attitude, for you may not be able to get back. For this reason porters are necessary on this death-defying trail. A small respite is given in the form of lovely birch and rhododendron forests which skirt the furious river. If you are very lucky you may spot the musk deer which inhabit these forests, or the Himalayan tatur leaping about the rock faces near Malatuni. Soon the trail peters out after the horrendous crossing of the Trisul Nala, another maelstrom, barring the way. Now the Rishi enters a box canyon and you have to start climbing up the sheer walls of the Rhamani slabs. One false step and the river is waiting with open jaws for another victim. Bhojgara marks the halfway stage of this perilous passage. More climbing and wriggling along the narrow ledges to outwit the

To enter the sanctuary the going can be very treacherous. This location just before Rhamani can be particularly so especially in the height of monsoons when the rocks offering foot and hand holds become slippery. Access, though difficult, is possible even with a minimum of equipment.

Page 103—Nanda Devi is seen at her best at sunrise and on a clear night with a full moon. The ridges and peaks making up her curtain protect her lower approaches and it is only when near her base camp that the viewer is privileged with a glimpse of the entire mountain.

river brings you to Tilchaunani, a camping site used by Shipton's party. The mountain looms ahead and is blocked by another impassable curtain of rock. The answer is more climbing to the modern camping site of Patalkhan. From here a level but distressing way across a mountain of unstable rocking boulders brings you to the undreamt of beauty of the South Inner Sanctuary. No explorer could wish for a more spectacular climax to the hazards of the way. The mountain rises serenely with coppery-green striations in its peak, glinting in the rarefied air. The Rishi parts into two streams at its feet as though in obeisance and all around are snow peaks, miles of rolling flower spangled emerald meadows running upto jagged moraines. Bharal, the wild blue sheep, graze in flocks, unafraid of men, but keeping a wary eye open for its enemy the snow leopard. Base camp lies another march ahead up the South Nanda Devi glacier at 5,338 m. From Deodhi one can climb north towards Dunagiri and Changabang base camps. From Trisul Nala lies access to Bethartoil and Trisul base camps. From Patalkhan another trail drops down to cross the Rishi river at Goofa camp site. This dangerous leap leads into the North Inner Sanctuary, the most spectacular area of them all, with a view of the tremendous north faces of the twin peaks, the *sanctum sanctorum* Nanda Devi.

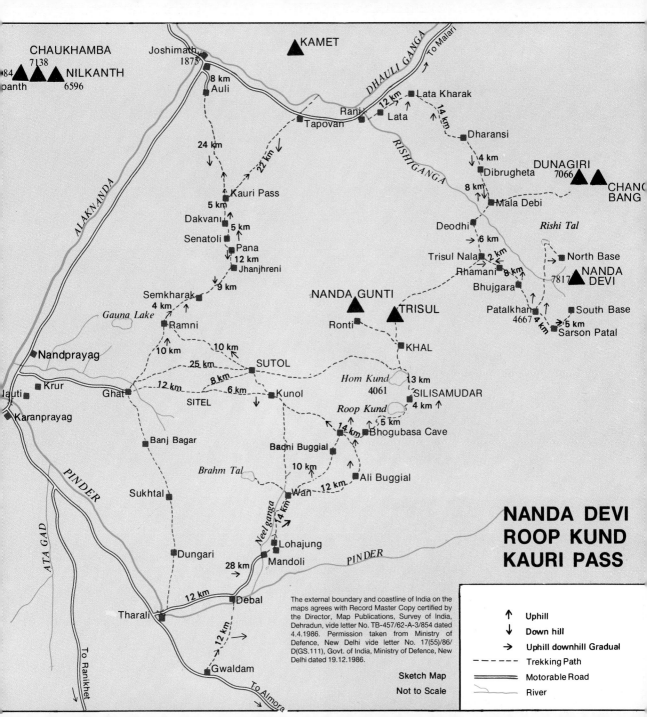

Above—From Kauri Pass one stands at the divide of the middle and greater Himalaya, towering peaks are a mere footstep away.

Left—The 'iron bell' at Lohajung rung to warn the local devta of a human presence. Nanda Ghunti peeks up over the ridge.

106

Curzon's Trail

Kauri Pass Trek

OFTEN known as the Curzon Trail, the trek to Kauri Pass is considered by many to be the most characteristically beautiful in the Garhwal Himalaya. Entry to the trail is made from Gwaldam though a shortened version is to start half-way along at Ghat. From Gwaldam the bridle path runs down steeply to cross the Pindar and gives an awesome close-up view of the three prongs of the trident mountain of Shiva, Trisul. Joining the motor road at Debal one follows the stream to Bakrighat then climbs steeply for a kilometer to Mundoli village and above it, the pass at Lohajung. This means "the rusted iron" and refers to the bell that hangs suspended from a cypress, to be rung to advise the *devta* (local spirit of the hilltop) that a visitor as arrived.

Now follows a lovely section along the wooded Neel Ganga to Wan, with a branch off on to the south to a small lake with trout at Brahm Tal, or north to the village of Didana and a very steep climb to the buggyal of Ali, *en route* to Roop Kund. Wan is a fascinating old village where the men and women continue to wear traditional Garhwali brown homespun wool blankets pinned across the chest.

From Wan you pass the sacred grove of Latu, another famous local *devta* whose temple lies under one of the biggest deodars in India, though now unfortunately snapped off at the top. The climb up through huge, magnificent cypress trees will warm the heart of the tree lover and the section from Wan to Sutol via the tiny clearing of Kunol will provide an elixir to any camper in the choice of marvellous camping sites. Wildlife still roams in these old, gnarled, full-grown virgin forests.

From Kunol one can exit to Ghat down through more magnificent conifer country via the bungalow on the riverside at Sitol, said by many to be the most beautifully sited rest house in the area. The Sutol to Ramni stretch is level and passes through a populated village area where the Ghat entry to the trail joins. From Ramni one has a steep climb to the wild jungle of Sem Kharak where the irridescent, multi-hued monal pheasant is still to be seen screaming downhill as the rustle of leaves disturbs his powerful digging claws. Then a steep descent to Jhenjhenipatni and the spectacular suspension bridge near the tiny village, slung across the Birehi gorge, one of the wildest spots imaginable.

You are now entering really rough country, for this river's higher reaches have not yet been explored. Look down and you see the Gauna lake which burst to flood the whole of Ganga valley down to Rishikesh in 1898.

The last village of Panarani announces the start of the backbreaking climb to the Pass. But the trail winds through such magnificently varied wild crag and forest scenery that you do not notice the exertion. The last haul up to the Kauri (which means "doorway") is almost vertical, from Dakwani, a shepherd's camping lodge. Passing through the horns of the Kauri you find some level ground to negotiate before you cross the rolling buggyals to the edge of the great divide between the Lesser and the Greater Himalaya. The blinding vision of the snow peaks makes all the effort worth its while, for this is beyond dispute one of the greatest mountain views in the world. Down at your feet lies Tapovan, a day's trek with the comfort of hot springs and a motor road awaiting you.

The terraced fields below the village of Debal are being harvested of their wheat. The triple-pronged peaks of Trisul overlook the valley.

Pages 110-111—Roop Kund, the cauldron-like grave of over 300 people exposes her secrets only during a warm wet year when the snow and ice on the lake are melted. Many travel to Roop Kund and go unrewarded finding only a vague snow-covered resemblance of a lake.

The Mystery Lake

Roop Kund

NOT one of the most beautiful lakes in Garhwal, but certainly one of the most fascinating, Roop Kund lies at an elevation of 4,778 m. Although fairly large in area, it is quite shallow, only six feet deep, 500 feet in circumference and covering an area of 2,000 sq yds. Its altitude and location, on the south face, preclude its thawing except for a few short weeks, after the summer heat and monsoon rains. What is it then that attracts so many trekkers to this place? Along the route is an excellent view of the Himalaya, Nanda Gunti, Trisul, Magtoli (east), Chaukhamba. Also, the buggyals crossed flower during most of the hiking season. But the biggest attraction is the mystery surrounding the lake. Over 300 people are believed to have met their untimely end here some 500-600 years ago. It is to see this grisly site of skeletal remains that many journey here. The mystery lake, as it is often called, continues to hold her secrets, only giving them up every few years during favourable warm, wet weather. Most who travel to Roop Kund go unrewarded and never view the remains of those who perished here, but the temptation is strong and many will continue to return year after year in the hope of a furtive glimpse of the freezer-like grave.

For many years, the mystery that the lake contained lay undiscovered. In 1942, a forest officer discovered the lake and bones. That was the beginning of the speculation. The further one goes from the site the more stories are heard. They range from Tibetan traders, to refugees fleeing from prosecution, to part of Tughlak's army under General Zowar Singh. Of these the best possibility would be the refugees. Tibetans never had a trade route here and none of the skeletons are mongoloid. The army theory is also unlikely. No weapons were found and if the army passed through, some record would have been made. Furthermore, there is no passage to Tibet in this area. There are too many difficult passes to cross to make these theories possible. Refugees might not travel by known routes but from what country did they flee?

According to *Dant Katha* (folkore/legend spoken or sung in ballad form), Raja Jasdal of Kanauj undertook a Nanda Jat 550 years ago, with his wife, Rani Balpa, and their two children. The Rani was a Garhwali Princess of Chandpur Garh and as such considered a sister of Nanda Devi, the patron goddess of Garhwal. So this special Nanda Jat was taken to propitiate Nanda Devi. Three or four kilometers below Roop Kund,

a lying-in-room called Rani-ka-suleda or Balpa-Suleda was built for the Rani. The ruins remain as testimony. Nanda Devi was angered that a child had been born on her holy land, polluting it, and sent a snow/hail storm down on this group. An advance party of the Raja continuing to Hom Kund, was caught while climbing the ridge, and presumably died from the fall or exposure. The protected area of Roop Kund provided a natural deep-freeze where the remains were protected from the elements as well as being preserved, where as the area of the Ranika-suleda is an open area and very few artifacts remain. According to the artifacts so far recovered this Nanda Jat explanation is the most viable. Copper plates recording the Jat, 500-600 years ago correspond to carbon dating by various groups. However the mystery remains and many people discuss the alternatives and seem to believe whichever theory strikes their fancy.

Hom Kund, 13 km beyond Roop Kund, is the goal for pilgrims involved in the Nanda Jat, or Raj Jat as it is also called because of the initial patronage of the Raja Ajai Pal of Garhwal in the fourteenth century. This event celebrates the marriage of Shiva and Parvati (Nanda). The Yatra is the bridal procession travelling from the bride's home to her in-law's. Seasonal changes, fertility rites and Hinduism are all interwoven. The Yatra route is slightly longer than the trekking route, and takes a leisurely pace, as befits a goddess, stopping at every village and every few kilometers to rest. After reaching Roop Kund the Yatra crosses the ridge where the fateful accident of the Raja of Kanauj took place. This ridge is called Jiura Gali, or the Valley of Destruction (Death). Villagers also associate this area with Rudra, the god of anger and tread carefully while here. It is no wonder that these associations are made. Many used to leave for Yatras never to return. The pilgrimage is completed barefoot from Bedni Buggyal to Hom Kund, an incredible feat since usually the area is covered in snow. The number of the pilgrims is variable with some dropping out according to desire and ability. But several thousand manage to cross and perform their puja at Hom Kund (Homkuni) where a Sri Yantra (tantric symbol) identical to the one at Nauti, is placed.

Smaller Raj Jats are taken annually from Krur and a smaller circuit is crossed. The *Barra* (grand) Raj Jat is supposed to occur every twelve years (September 1984 was the scheduled date) when a four-horned ram

One of the few ways to get warm also brings with it the uncomfortable sting of smoke. Porters, though used to the cold, willingly risk this in order to be seated near its warmth.

Facing page—Grazing at Ali Buggyal are sheep from the nearby village of Wan. Villagers depend on these animals for their clothing as well as money with which to purchase necessities which cannot grow at this altitude. Extensive terracing is feasible only at lower altitudes making the purchase of staples necessary.

is born. At Hom Kund, the ram, loaded with saddlebags filled with offerings for the goddess, leaves the party continuing on to Nanda Devi. The British scoffed at the idea of the 'natives' climbing to such heights but the proof lies waiting, for those who journey to Roop Kund. The Raj Jat took place in August 1987.

Roop Kund Trek

Options:

1. Gwaldom or Tharali to Debal return
2. Gwaldom/Tharali Roop Kund Hom kund-Ghat
3. Kauri Pass via Roop Kund Hom Kund

Tharali to Debal is 12 km along a sometimes motorable road; check and see if trucks or jeeps are travelling along the road, (it is possible to take transport until just below Mundoli), as it is a hot walk.

Gwaldom to Debal is also 12 km but here the path gradually descends then ascends after meeting the road from Tharali. Along the road it is 26 km to Mundoli but there are several shortcuts, be on the look-out for them. Approximately 3 km below Mundoli the road begins its zigzag climb and here a shortcut heads straight up the river valley. From Mundoli it is a 2 km steep ascent to Lohajung where the Tourist Bungalow is located. Wan lies 14 km away along a path that gradually descends then gradually ascends. To Bedni Buggyal first the path descends 2 km and crosses the Neel Ganga then it is a 8 km steep climb. From Bedni Buggyal Pater Nachani is 12 km; the path is described as "straight" meaning small ups and downs. From here to Kailu Binaik (Ganesh Murti) is a 3 km steep ascent. Then straight to Bhogubasa Cave for less than a kilometer. To Roop Kund it is a 5 km steep ascent. If there is snow ice axes will be useful, especially if the snow is crusty. If continuing on, it is 4 km steep ascent then steep descent to Silisamunder. Hom Kund lies 13 km beyond here. Another 8 km is Homkund Khal (Ronti Saddle) which is Trisul south face base camp. From Homkund to Sutol is 8 km then to Ghat via Sitol or straight out (a distance of more than 25 km but people seem to disagree about how far exactly).

Note

It is possible to do this trek (Roop Kund return trip) without a tent (we did) but be prepared to rough it at Bhogabasa Cave and at Bedni Buggyal.

The Towns of Garhwal

Dehra Dun

SITUATED near the middle of the valley popularly called the Dun valley, Dehra Dun has been typically associated with the very young and the old. An old saying around town states that Dehra Dun is the place for schools, (the young), and a place to retire, (the old). Its moderate climate lacking the extremes found in the plains and in the hill stations provides year-round comfort. The Indian Military Academy is the most prominent of the various educational institutions with the Doon School running a close second since it is the Prime Minister, Rajiv Gandhi's alma mater.

Dehra Dun is the railhead for the area with direct trains connecting it with Delhi, Bombay and Calcutta (and points in between). An airport with connections to all major cities provides faster transportation, and the bus service, especially to Delhi, is fast and reliable.

Dehra Dun began as the center for Guru Ram Rai and his followers when the Maharaja of Garhwal, Fateh Shah welcomed him to the valley in 1699 (Guru Ram Rai retreated here after failing to succeed his father as Guru). A Gurudwara was constructed and to maintain it the Maharaja gave the Guru five villages to tax to provide funds. Gradually devotees and followers built around the Gurudwara creating Dehra Dun (dehra meaning staying place or staying valley).

Mussoorie

The British built Mussoorie originally as a convalescence hill station. The oldest house belonging to Captain Young, built in 1829, still stands below Landour. The early visitors came from Saharanpur to Rajpur by cart then walked or were carried up via Barlowganj. The town straggling along ten miles of a ridge, views the Great Himalaya on the north side and the verdant Dun Valley south-wards. Here also was marked the last fix on the Great Trig Survey of India. The man who surveyed the sub-continent, George Everest, lived in Mussorie from 1832 to 1843, and his house, with the local gossip about its Bibi-khana, a harem building, can still be viewed. The name Mussoorie came from a local shrub and prior to the sahibs and shikaris, no one came here except cowherds. Soon the town attracted a bewildering variety of visitors and must today rank as one of the most cosmopolitan towns outside the U.N. Building. Being neither the summer capital of the provincial or central govern-

Above—The Mussoorie area is a vantage point for both the Yamuna and the Ganga. The watershed divide for these holy rivers runs through the town.

Left—Typical of all hill-stations is a view of the snows. Mussoorie straddles a horse-shoe shaped ridge above the Dehra Dun valley.

115

ment, Mussoorie (being nearer to Delhi than either Simla or Nainital) could afford to let its hair down. Its reputation of a gay, fun-loving station lasted till the British left India. Hakman's on the Mall was included in the itinerary of cabaret artists who made the rounds of Monte Carlo and Las Vegas.

At the east end is Landour cantonment and in the west is the old Library. Linking them is the Mall which passes through the main shopping centre of Kulri. If you stop and look at the old buildings in the heart of the town like the old Imperial Bank building opposite the post office (now the State Bank), you can see the wrought iron grilles with the insignia of Queen Victoria. Other old associations are the lamp posts manufactured in Glasgow and still giving good service after a hundred years. Mussoorie is a convenient base for treks to the interior, and roads from here lead to the sources of the Ganga and the Yamuna to the north, as well as to Tehri in the east and Simla in the west.

Most people prefer Mussoorie as the nearest place from Delhi to beat the heat for a weekend. The season is short but hectic and several cinema halls and roller-skating rinks are crowded with the young set, while their elders are content to promenade along the Mall. Mussoorie may have lost some of its style but none of its reputation of being a free and fun-loving hill-station.

Joshimath

The town of Joshimath has uncharitably been described as an over-grown shanty-town. It certainly has none of the elegance of its sister hill resorts in the lower and more easily accessible regions of Garhwal, but it has a charm and beauty in keeping with its prestigious honour of being both the *math* for the *dham*, Badrinath and for being the site where the famous Adiguru Shankaracharya attained enlightenment before beginning his campaign for the unification of India and the revitalisation of Hinduism.

The Nar Singh temple is the seat of the Rawal of Badrinath during the winter and is an integral part of the legend surrounding the Badris. The statue of Nar Singh is the determining factor in the final closing of the Badrinath temple and the opening of the new temple at *Bhavisya* Badri near Tapovan. Legend proclaims that when the arm of the Nar Singh idol finally breaks, (it's been getting smaller every year), the road to Badrinath will be blocked and the new Badri will open.

Joshimath is the staging ground for the continuing journey to Badrinath. It is from here that the one-way road begins and the town plays host to those waiting for the gate (as the traffic is called) and for those stranded by the closing of the gate for the night. As such, several accomodations have sprung up and with time this town will soon emulate its sister hill-resorts, except possibly with a little more charm.

Joshimath is the base for several treks. It is also the best place to engage porters because of the quantity available and the experience they collectively have. If you need porters who have been to a particular area and who have experience of trekking tell one and they will determine who is the best to acccompany the trek.

A ski resort is under construction in the meadows of Auli and Gorson 9 km from Joshimath. It is currently open with limited facilities.

Uttarkashi

This small town along the route to Gangotri is slowly gaining importance as a center in the Garhwal with the construction of several universities and the Nehru Institute of Mountaineering. The institute provides instruction in mountaineering as well as helping organise, sponsor, and supply various trekking groups and mountaineering expeditions. Tents, back-packs and other equipment can be rented directly from the institute or from other agencies in Uttarkashi.

Treks from here are the Gangotri region, Dodi Tal, Yamunotri (via Dodi Tal), the Sahastra Tal region, and the old Kedarnath yatra route. Foreigners must register here in order to travel in most of the areas.

Srinagar

When speaking about the towns of Garhwal chronologically, we find Srinagar still the cultural capital, with the new hill university campus sited in the open valley, the widest in Garhwal, alongside the Ganga. Srinagar was the third medieval capital of Garhwal, founded soon after Chandpur and Dewalgarh, probably in the fifteenth century. The name is associated with a tantric device, the Sri Yantra, which is said to be so powerful that Shankaracharya, the great philosopher and founder of the orthodox Hindu shrines of Garhwal, turned it upside down where it can still be seen as a rock in the river. From the sixteenth century Srinagar had a flourishing court life and its miniature paintings are accounted amongst the finest in the Pahari schools. Unfortunately, floods and earthquakes in 1894-1898 stripped Srinagar of its glory and now hardly any old buildings remain.

Tehri

In 1815, as the price of evicting the Nepali invaders from Garhwal, the Maharaja agreed to cede his territory East of the Alaknanda (Ganga) to the British. This meant relinquishing his seat at Srinagar. In the hot valley of Tehri, the Maharaja rebuilt his capital and the story goes that when the British resident made a suprise visit, a special guesthouse (more like a palace) was constructed in the space of a few days. Alas, this town which preserved the flavour of the old Garhwal, is now due to be submerged by the Tehri Dam scheme, the biggest of its kind in Asia. The palace will disappear and the

117

bazaar shopkeepers will be relocated higher on the hill near Chamba. The villagers will be given land in the foothills, but in spite of all this there is much local resistance to this wholesale dislocation of Garhwali culture.

Narendranagar

Due to the extreme heat, the Garhwal Maharaja built a summer capital, actually a palace, on the way to Tehri from Rishikesh. This is Narendranagar which is visible from the plains. This palace became famous in the world of art for here were to be found collections of the finest miniature paintings which experts had supposed to be confined to the western Himalayan princely states. Apparently the famous Raja Sansar Chand of Kangra, worried at the expanding Sikh influence in Himachal, married his daughters into the Hindu royal family of Garhwal. The Maharaja of Garhwal has always been the traditional custodian of the sacred shrines of Badrinath and Kedarnath.

Pauri

Following the 1815 agreement with the British, the area east of the Ganga became known as Pauri Garhwal after the small town was developed by the British to be their administrative centre. Pauri lies on the Kotdwar-Srinagar road (actually sited above Srinagar) and has a magnificent view of the snows. Pauri became in 1960 the administrative headquarters of the new division of Garhwal. Formerly the British had included Pauri Garhwal in the Kumaon division and this had led to considerable confusion amongst visitors who may not be aware of the traditional rivalry—a War of the Roses situation—that exists between the people of Kumaon and Garhwal. The British built a bridle path connecting Pauri with Almora and this old trail winding for days (of double stages) in full view of the snow peaks, passes through unspoiled forests and enables the visitor to see the traditional lifestyle of these hill regions.

Lansdowne

South of Pauri on the way to Kotdwar lies the fascinating little town of Lansdowne, named after a Viceroy of the Victorian era. The tiny bazaar remains a good example of what the old hill stations looked like under the British. The town is famous as the home town of the Garhwal Rifles, a doughty infantry regiment that specialised in acquiring the rare and coveted Victoria Cross, the highest military decoration—and the plainest: the bronze medal on a purple ribbon reads simply "For Valour". Lansdowne has fine views of both the snows and the plains but like so many other hill stations, with the felling of the trees, it has begun to suffer from shortage of water.

Chakrata

In the far west of Garhwal is another favourite small hill station of the British, Chakrata, on the way to Simla from Mussoorie or Dehra Dun. The view of the snows from the neighbouring hill was considered so beautiful by the British that they had a picture of it printed officially (by the Survey of India) for sale to the public and this is still available. The surrounding area is culturally fascinating, as the villagers practise polyandry. It is also rich in ancient associations and at Kalsi can be seen the fine example of the edict of Emperor Ashoka, carved on a polished boulder around 250 BC and rediscovered accidently by a British traveller some two thousand years later.

A Delicate Environment

The Himalaya are undoubtedly one of the most imposing physical features on earth. From a distance they appear unassailable and inspire a sense of eternity. But even though they might seem to stand above the threat of human depredation, the Himalaya are intensely fragile, a complex environment which depends on many different facets of nature for its survival. Because of the extreme differences in altitude and the relative youthfulness of the mountains, they are more vulnerable to change. At the same time, the Himalaya contain many valuable resources such as forests, water, minerals, medicinal herbs, pastures, etc. Human beings have lived in these regions for centuries and learned to use these resources carefully and without waste, but with the pressures of population and the rapacious exploitation by forest contractors, quarry owners and dam engineers, the delicate balances of nature have been destroyed. Large areas of the mountains have been denuded through wanton felling of oak and evergreen forests. Entire ridges have been stripped bare by limestone mining. Rivers have been choked by ill-planned hydro-electric schemes.

But what can a lonely trekker do to help protect and conserve the Himalaya? Certainly, in the face of such monstrous abuse, his week-long hike seems hardly an intrusion on nature. Greater forces of destruction are at work and the boot which tramples a flower seems insignificant when compared to a charge of dynamite which can shatter a hillside. The trekker avoids the sight of disfigured mountains and ravaged valleys, preferring to search out the untouched forests and unblemished snow of the higher Himalaya.

Even though the trekker may content himself with the knowledge that there are others who are committing far greater offences against nature, this does not absolve him from a certain responsibility. The trekker must carry with him an attitude of conservation, an appreciation not just for the challenge and exertion of the trek, but for nature itself. This awareness of birds, flowers, ferns, lichens and trees makes the trek a much more valuable experience and helps the trekker to understand the environment through which he is passing. Once he understands something of his surroundings, the trekker will think twice before he hacks down a sapling which got in the way of his tent or shifts a boulder to make a more comfortable seat. He will realize that the sapling may seem small and insignificant but it represents a whole new generation of trees. The boulder may be a lifeless mass but underneath it there is a whole colony of insects and other tiny creatures who must now evacuate their homes and find another

Above—What is the obligation of a visitor to the Himalaya? The lack of consideration shown by many is obvious.

Left—The Himalayan Birch faces possible extinction because of the careless disregard when gathering fuel.

Following page—Tread carefully and courteously.

Page 123—The Kalimath temple 6 km from Guptakashi is the site of a large Bhagwati temple. A festival is held annually with pilgrims travelling from throughout the country to be here. Ritual sacrifices are still commonly practised here.

stone under which to live all because of a thoughtless trekker who wanted to rest his tired hindquarters.

These examples may seem exaggerated but the scatterings of litter, tins, bottles, paper and plastic which have begun to decorate some of the more popular campsites in the Himalaya are obvious reminders of the insensitivity which all human beings exhibit towards nature. Only a conscious effort can help conserve these mountains and each individual must take that responsibility.

Garhwal has always been a place of pilgrimage and for centuries outsiders have walked along the many beautiful trails that cross these mountains. Despite all of the dams, mining operations and felled forests, Garhwal still has many hidden valleys and untrampled meadows.

The trekker should approach these shrines of nature as a pilgrim, with a sense of reverence and awe.

Useful Phrases in Hindi/Garhwali

Questions

Where is..............? Kahan hai...........?
How many km is...........? Kitne km..............hai?
Does this bus/road/path go...? Kya yeh gari/rasta ....jata hai?
Where can I find (food)? (Khanna) kahan milta hai?

Words/Answers

One	*ek*	village	*gaon*
Two	*doe*	upper	*oopar*
Three	*teen*	down/below	*neechay*
Four	*char*	ahead	*aagay*
Five	*panch*	behind	*peechay*
Six	*chhay*	old man	*boda*
Seven	*saat*	old woman	*bodi*
Eight	*aath*	(same age) man	*bhai-ji*
Nine	*naw*	(same age)	*didi*
Ten	*dus*	woman	
Eleven	*gyara*	boy	*bulla*
Twelve	*baara*	girl	*bulli*
Twenty	*bese*	good/O.K.	*atcha teekhai*
Fifty	*pachas*	bad	*kharab*
Hundred	*saw*	hot	*garam*
		cold	*thanda*
Bus/taxi	*gari*	water	*panni*
medicine	*dawa*	milk	*doodh*
tea	*chai*	rice	*bhaat*
food	*khanna*	flour	*atta*
rope	*rassi*	cooking oil	*ghee*
right (direction)	*sidha or dhain*		
left	*ulta or bahin*		

Advice and Helpful Hints

1. These treks are for those who can think on their feet. Descriptions are vague to encourage individual choice. Campsites abound and would be too numerous to mention. However certain portions that should be completed in one day or when water should be carried have been mentioned.

2. "Straight" is a relative term. It may mean that the path begins and ends at the same elevation or that small hills lie between.

3. In the hills ask for directions three times, keep asking until the story matches; people often answer without knowing what they're talking about.

4. Some beautiful locations have received little or no attention. This is an attempt to keep treasure hunters/destroyers away from the area. These spots are there for anyone willing to seek them out.

5. Porters are useful not only for carrying extra loads but they will gather wood and build a fire if and when necessary, make tea (ration the sugar), cook food, and wash the dishes (or nappies!). Some are temperamental but the good ones are well "worth their weight in GOLD".

Glossary

Ashram—dwelling of a rishi or sadhu, who generally provides lodge and board to pilgrims

Badri—berry, referring to the fruit eaten by Vishnu

Bhagiratha—the sage who mediated at Gangotri in order to bring the holy Ganga down

Brahma—the first of the Hindu Gods, known as the Creator

Buggyal—High altitude meadow

Chatti—eating and lodging place

Darshan—to view and to be in the presence of the deity

devta—minor god or deity

dham—a holy place; Shankaracharya established four in India, Badrinath Puri(Orissa), Dwarka, (Gujarat), and Rameshwaram(Tamil Nadu). The four dhams of the Himalaya are Yamunotri, Gangotri, Kedarnath, Badrinath

Dharamshala—a resting place, generally free or at low rates, or asking only for donations

dun—a valley

dwar—gate or entrance

Ganesh—the Elephant-headed. Hindu God of Wisdom, son of Shiva and Parvati. Appealed to at the start of any new venture because he is the remover of obstacles.

Garh—fort

Ghat—a flat land generally beside a river used for various purposes, bathing, cremation

Gujjar—Nomadic people who own cows, buffaloes and goats graze them in the upper Himalaya during summer and return to the plains nearby in winter

Gurudwara—the worship place of the Sikhs

Hanuman—Monkey God possessing great strength

Kamandal—a vessel for containing water or other things

Kedarkhand—the land of divine attainments and eternal peace, Shiva's abode

Kauravas—the hundred brothers who were slain by the Pandavas because of their wicked ways, in the battle of Kurukshetra

Kund—a pond, pool or lake

Lakshman—the brother of Rama

Lingam—the phallic symbol associated with Shiva, formerly worshipped in fertility cults

Mahabharata—an epic through which the fundamental teachings of Hinduism are portrayed to the common people.

Moksha—deliverance from the cycle of birth and death

Pandavas—Five hero brothers of the epic *Mahabharata* who killed the Kauravas: Yudhishthira, Bhim, Arjun, Nakula, Sahadeva, their common wife, Draupadi

Parvat—mountain

prasad—Blessed sweets or other items received after worship

prayag— a sacred confluence of rivers

Puja—worship

Raga-Ragini—Musical tones and series

Rishi—a Hindu saint

Sage—wise man

Sanskrit—ancient Indian language, the Vedas were composed in this language

Shiva—the third God of the Hindu trinity, the destroyer. He is worshipped in the form of Lingam

Tantra—a method of achieving occult powers, two schools, the left-handed associated with evil and the other, simply called tantra.

Uttra Khand—uttra-north; khand-region; referring to the northern districts of Garhwal, the location of many holy shrines

Vedas—books of knowledge ascribed to the Aryans, composed in hymn-form containing information on a wide range of subjects

Vishnu—the second God in the Hindu Trinity, the preserver.

Yatra—a journey to a holy place

Yatri—a pilgrim

Index